AF776953

Praise for *A Matter of Hope*

"This is the book you need to read at this moment in our world. Instead of allowing the personal pain he's experienced to be an excuse to turn away from life's hardest challenges, Jim Bildner embraces them with a fierceness that is breathtaking. With real examples, he offers hard-won, practical advice on tackling the problems most of us assume are unsolvable in our lifetimes—child hunger on the African continent, the high rate of recidivism in America's prisons. The ingredient that must infuse all this work is hope, he insists, and when you put the book down, you'll have a lot more of it."

—Judy Woodruff, former Anchor, *PBS News Hour*;
Peabody Award Winner; and Nationally and Internationally
Acclaimed Journalist

"Hope isn't wishful thinking—it's built on a foundation of belief in the essential humanity in each of us. Jim Bildner's very life journey, and the powerful examples in his uplifting book, reinforce—or restores—our confidence in the future. A great read at a critical time in our nation."

—General Stanley McChrystal, US Army, Retired;
CEO and Chairman McChrystal Group

"As an entrepreneur, CEO, company builder, and investor, I am in awe over what Jim and his team at DRK have achieved. In this book, Jim describes their work and true achievements, and offers a crisp playlist for current and new entrepreneurs in building scalable and successful social impact enterprises. It's a must-read."

—Tim Koogle, former CEO and Chairman, Yahoo!;
former Chairman and Investor, Method;
and Chairman, Ripple Foods, OllyPBC

"Jim and DRK have been rising to the challenges of our time and creating different destinies for millions of people since I have known them. *A Matter of Hope* is one of those singular books you cannot put down. From tears of joy to goosebumps while you read—Jim shows us how literally anyone can move hope to action. For funders it's not just a playbook; it's a must-read on what it takes to create change in the world. It's our go-to playbook."

—Carrie Morgridge, CEO and Cofounder,
Morgridge Family Foundation; Author,
Every Gift Matters, The Spirit of the Trail,
and *Courage Money*

"*A Matter of Hope* tells the stories of a wide range of heroic people who dedicated themselves to making the world a better place. The point, though, is not that these individuals are extraordinary but that we can all be extraordinary this way if we just believe in ourselves, our ideas, and the possibilities of a better future. And Jim should know, as he has done it himself, and here he offers practical advice as well as inspiration about how each of us can find opportunities that draw on our own passions and experience to do something truly meaningful."

—Larry Kramer, President and Vice Chancellor,
London School of Economics and Political Science;
former President, William and Flora Hewlett Foundation;
former Dean, Stanford Law School

"For more than three decades I have seen challenge after challenge in the world. I have also seen time and time again, the power of the human heart and mind surmount these challenges. In every case, these people saw the world not with all its flaws but with all its potential. The ability to harness hope as an anchor for change has transformed my life and I know it will do the same for you."

—Sue Gordon, Former Principal Deputy Director of
National Intelligence; President, GordonVentures, LLC

"I know first hand that hope and belief in a better future are the building block for making change happen. Throughout my life, I have seen this belief enable people to overcome fear and resignation and unlock their potential to make a difference. Jim's book is the playbook to making this happen."

—Ruth Simmons, former President of Spellman,
Brown University, and Texas Prairie A&M University;
Bestselling Author; and Multiple Prize Winner
including the National Humanities Medal

"Jim Bildner is a leader who makes a difference in the world. His new book, *A Matter of Hope*, is the playbook for social entrepreneurs and funders on how change takes place in communities and the world. And for impact investors, it shows why venture philanthropy is so vital to creating innovative interventions that address some of the world's most pressing challenges."

—Rob Kaplan, Vice Chair, Goldman Sachs; former President,
Dallas Federal Reserve; Leadership Professor,
Harvard Business School; and Author,
What You Really Need to Lead,
What You're Really Meant To Do,
and *What to Ask the Person in the Mirror*

"This book is the primer on social innovation and entrepreneurship. Each story offers a powerful nugget of wisdom that can be applied to everyone's journey of impact. As the CEO of Draper Richards Kaplan Foundation, Jim Bildner not only knows the craft of supporting entrepreneurs but he himself has been a consummate entrepreneur. Over the past thirteen years, he has led our foundation to the next level of finding, funding, and supporting great entrepreneurs. You will learn all the best skills about the practice from a consummate practitioner."

—Robin Richards Donohoe, Founder and Managing Director,
Draper International, Draper Richards Funds

"Jim Bildner's *A Matter of Hope* is full of stories of inspiring social entrepreneurs, some of whom I've had the privilege to meet personally. They share how hope has enabled them to overcome their fears and remain tenacious in the face of adversity. It is also an amazing playbook for entrepreneurs to deeply understand the problem they are trying to solve, articulate their end game, and then identify the best execution strategy, leveraging the ecosystem, resources, and available partners.

It is a must read for funders who want to use venture philanthropy to create scalable social ventures—backing the right people with multi-year, unrestricted funding and also supporting the ventures to succeed with capability and community.

Jim's own profound life experiences have illustrated that time is precious and how you spend your time matters most, and this book is a very worthy investment of time!"

—Jessica Mendoza-Roth, Founder and CEO, Social Impact Hub

A MATTER OF HOPE

Lessons Learned from Leaders, Changemakers, and Visionaries on Making a Difference in the World

JIM BILDNER

Matt Holt Books
An Imprint of BenBella Books, Inc.
Dallas, TX

A Matter of Hope copyright © 2026 by Jim Bildner

All rights reserved. Except in the case of brief quotations embodied in critical articles or reviews, no part of this book may be reproduced, stored, transmitted, or used in any manner whatsoever, including for training artificial intelligence (AI) technologies or for automated text and data mining, without prior written permission from the publisher.

Matt Holt is an imprint of BenBella Books, Inc.
BenBella Books, Inc.
8080 N. Central Expressway
Suite 1700
Dallas, TX 75206
benbellabooks.com
Send feedback to feedback@benbellabooks.com

Matt Holt and *BenBella* are federally registered trademarks.

Printed in the United States of America
10 9 8 7 6 5 4 3 2 1

Library of Congress Control Number: 2026013896
ISBN 9781637749760 (hardcover)
ISBN 9781637749777 (electronic)

Editing by Katie Dickman
Copyediting by Michael Fedison
Proofreading by Mary White and Denise Pangia
Indexing by WordCo. Indexing Services
Text design and composition by Jordan Koluch
Cover design by Jason Arias
Cover image © Adobe Stock / PeterSchreiber.Media
Printed by Lake Book Manufacturing

Special discounts for bulk sales are available.
Please contact bulkorders@benbellabooks.com.

To my three granddaughters,
Ruth, Ava, and Grace, who light up my life with endless hope and joy and belief in the future. Poppy will always love you for who you are and who you will become.

Contents

"Everyone, and I mean everyone, has the ability to make a difference in someone's life . . . if they choose to act."

—Jim Bildner

Foreword

by William H. Draper III

Over the course of eight decades as an entrepreneur, a venture capitalist, a public servant, and a husband and father, I have seen firsthand the power of hope in changing the lives of millions.

In 2011, I wrote *The Startup Game*, a book about how entrepreneurs can change the world through bold ideas, relentless execution, and powerful partnerships. Much of what I wrote about then, derived from my decades in the venture capital community, I saw over and over again, entrepreneurs creating new pathways and technologies that have forever changed the way we live. In the venture capital world, economic return was the measurement that mattered. But in the venture philanthropy and impact investing world, what matters is social return—making a difference in the lives of others. What I learned then—and what I know more certainly now—is that the characteristic that enables leaders to create these impactful organizations that change the lives of others is their inherent belief in the power of one human being to make a difference in the life of another. It's the fundamental ability to carry hope when others see despair, to imagine a future that does not yet exist, and to make it so, through thick and thin. I saw this commitment to making a difference in the lives of others when I ran the United Nations Development Programme, traveling to more than 100 countries to support programs that could reduce poverty, increase access to the basics of life, and promote sustainable growth. I saw this as well through my father when he helped operationalize the Marshall Plan after WWII to help Western Europe recover from the devastation of the war.

At DRK, this translated into investing in leaders who wore their commitment on their sleeve. I will never forget meeting John Wood, who had just started Room to Read after leaving his position as Microsoft's director of business development. John saw that literacy was a global problem and wanted to solve for it. Before I met with him, I asked him to bring a business plan to our meeting—no one had asked him for that yet.

When I came to his office, I saw piles and piles of books and a sleeping bag on the floor. When I asked him about it, he told me he had stayed up all night to create the business plan. It was clear to me that this was someone completely committed to his cause—an entrepreneur in every sense, giving everything to his mission. This early sign of commitment continued for decades. Today, Room to Read has brought education programs to more than 60 million children in 29 countries. And John is the rule, not the exception.

When I was asked to write this foreword, my response was simple: "Why did it take you so long to ask me?" Hope and the belief in a better future have anchored my life. And I know they will anchor yours.

Thank you, Jim, for putting into words my life's playbook. As they say, I am all in.

—William H. Draper III

Prologue: Making the Next Point Count

"It's about the power of one person to make a difference in the life of another."

—Jim Bildner, CEO, DRK

Each year for the Draper Richards Kaplan Foundation Annual Retreat, we bring together more than 120 of the 275 social entrepreneurs from our portfolio of organizations that we have invested in. They come from the United States and around the world. We ask the newest members to come the day before everyone else arrives, to share a moment in time together.

As the leaders of these newest DRK organizations enter the room, the energy is palpable. Though they are new DRK portfolio organizations, we know each and every one of them well, having spent months in diligence prior to investing in them—working side by side with them and their teams to understand who they are and what problems their organizations are trying to solve in the world.

As they gather around the tables in the room, we ask each of them to introduce themselves by sharing *what brought them to this work* and *what keeps them doing the work*—because we know it's likely the hardest job they've ever had.

Each of them describes it a bit differently, but there's no mistaking it. They all share an unrelenting belief in a better future and have an endless supply of hope that gets them through the challenges they inevitably face along the way. Without it, they wouldn't be able to do this work. It would just be too hard.

What we get is a juxtaposition. A room filled with discussions of life's many challenges, its inequities, adverse experiences, constraints, disappointments, and loss—the very things that have stopped others from doing this work—but also a room filled with a belief that the world can be so much better and that they are the folks that can make this happen.

Inside the room, there is a visceral sense of hope and purpose—the forces that have singularly allowed each of these changemakers to take the bad and turn it into a force for good, powered by a vision of how things might be.

It's the same power that has enabled our portfolio organizations, collectively, to impact more than 600 million lives, a number that grows every year by more than 100 million. During that meeting, something equally profound emerged. Most of the entrepreneurs stood up and said they came to the work because, at some point in their lives, the ability to be "in service" to others had fulfilled a longing to have purpose and meaning, in a world where purpose and meaning can be hard to find. But something else kept coming up—that this being in service to others filled a personal need. As each person spoke, one after another, over the course of two and a half hours, something surprising and powerful revealed itself. While their job fulfilled a deep sense of meaning, it also was *healing* each person in a way I hadn't fully appreciated. The simple act of helping another person was the antidote to healing their own vulnerabilities, fears, self-doubts, and the temptation to think that they are helpless.

This realization has stuck with me.

Hope *enabling* people to feel powerful at a time when they feel powerless is what this book is all about. Hope *allowing* people to override their fears.

Hope *inspiring* folks to move beyond their self-doubts and feeling like they are "impostors" in order to free them up to act and make a difference in the lives of others. Viewed in this context, I saw that hope is not something nice to have—it's a necessity. It's like the air we breathe. It gets us from today to tomorrow. It helps us persevere when things are difficult and survive when things are traumatic. I know this personally and from the hundreds of social entrepreneurs that I work with. And what has been reinforced over my 70+ years of life, and especially from the work I have done over the last 20 years, is that hope changes lives—millions of lives.

From working with hundreds of people on some of the most intractable problems on the ground, I've come to see that in each and every one of them—and in all of us—lies the potential to harness this profound sense of belief in a better tomorrow into tangible acts that in turn become solutions that make a huge difference in the lives of others. This deeply resonates with me as my own lived experience has been tried by moments where hope seemed elusive and the "siren song" of despair was not far away.

In December 2005, my wife, Nancy, and I got the call that is every parent's greatest fear. A Palm Beach sheriff was on the phone to let us know that our 21-year-old son, Peter, had died of a drug overdose—an addiction he had been battling for years that had finally consumed him. The detective who found our son's body told me that the addiction epidemic gripping the country is "a problem too big to be fixed, sir." "Try not to think about it," he said, as he gave me the number of the county morgue. But the truth is I couldn't stop thinking about it, not for a minute.

The detective was just stating a fact and a belief that he had gotten used to—that the problems of the world are unsolvable or too big and too painful to tackle. Four weeks after my son died, I recorded an op-ed that appeared on every public radio station across the United States on NPR's *Morning Edition*, entitled "Anyone's Son."[1] More than half a million people heard the piece and thousands reached out to me because my message struck a chord with them. My message in the piece then—and now—is the same. The problems of the world are our problems to be fixed. In 2005, it was my son, but if this problem persists, the next time, it could be yours.

My experience then was not unique. No parent imagines receiving that call. Events challenge our

---

1 Jim Bildner, "Accepting the Reality of Drug Addiction," NPR, June 6, 2006, www.npr.org/2006/06/06/5453486/accepting-the-reality-of-drug-addiction.

belief system all the time, often without warning. They affect everyone regardless of our perceived differences. It's something we see time and time again. But too often it paralyzes us, making us unable to see beyond the moment, beyond the abyss. And yet it doesn't have to be this way. I've seen example after example of people who recognize the reality of what's transpiring, but are able to move beyond it to find solutions that make a difference in the here and now.

I know firsthand how strange it is the way the world keeps moving after something so painful happens. Emails still arrive. The phone still rings. Another day begins and the normal routine of others' lives continues as if what happened to you never happened. The earth turns, the sun still shines, traffic flows, the everyday aspects of life continue unabated.

I had known my son was struggling—his addiction had carved deep wounds in our lives—and while I feared that inevitably his addiction would get the best of him, I never thought it would actually happen and so soon. These are moments you think will break you completely. That the construct you built your life around is shattered. This was that moment for us.

Over the decades that followed I realized I could never fit all those pieces back together. Instead, I had to reshape the world I was living in into something different. Because the truth is, I was different.

I began to see things I had never noticed before.

I started noticing that the world is full of tiny mercies—early morning sunlight on the ocean, the sound of seagulls welcoming the day, friends whose care is ever-present, strangers who donate to causes they'll never benefit from.

Then, 15 years after Peter's passing, we learned my wife, Nancy, had stage 4 metastatic cancer with a life expectancy of six months. I had already learned that life doesn't always bother with fairness. I held her hand while the doctors talked about treatment options and timelines. The same hand I held when we vowed "in sickness and in health," the same hand I held when our children were born.

And yet, miracles do occur. More than 80 chemo cycles and two clinical trials later, Nancy is still with me. I am still holding her hand, and she is holding mine.

By the time Nancy was diagnosed in 2021, I had been the CEO of the Draper Richards Kaplan Foundation, one of the world's largest global venture philanthropy organizations, for more than eight years. A role I still hold today. It's an organization that finds, funds, and supports social impact entrepreneurs—people who take on the problems most feel are too big and too complex to solve: clean water in rural communities, educational programs for kids who've been forgotten by the system, equitable access to health care, employment opportunities to end generational poverty, new markets for farmers to sell their products and make a better living, and so much more.

Before these personal storms, I had approached my life and my work with a belief that I was in control of life, that I could predict it. I approached it with a sense that life is unlimited. That time has no bounds. That today leads to tomorrow and tomorrow leads to the next day. But grief reprogrammed something in me.

I learned quickly that I was not in control. That time is precious and how you spend it matters. Before Peter died, I was consumed by my professional life. It set my priorities and how I spent my time. Boy, was I wrong. The things I missed in those years took me decades to recover. I missed so many of my daughter Lizzie's high school games, her birthday parties, carpooling her friends. While those moments were lost, I learned that they were not lost forever. That I could change. And I did. I became a "Ball Dad" for Lizzie's Dartmouth field hockey team—actually, the Captain of the "Ball Dads"—and never missed a game again. Thank you, Lizzie, for letting me back into your life. Next to your mother, you have anchored my life more than anyone.

Jim Bildner

Jim Bildner, Captain "Ball Dad," and daughter Lizzie at a Dartmouth field hockey match.

I also learned what real purpose means—it's how and what you do for others that matters. And that, at the end of the day, doing for others is all that matters. It defines a life. Instantly I saw things I had never really seen before and dedicated my work to making a difference in the lives of others.

As I said at my son's memorial service, how ironic it was that someone like me who wanted to save the world couldn't save his own son.

The truth was, I wasn't looking or listening hard enough. But I am now and I have been for more than two decades. I started listening—really listening—and I started looking harder, noticing the life around me.

And what have I seen?

I have seen the schoolchildren in Nairobi, Kenya,

and in Oakland, California, who can now learn and thrive in school because they are given nutritious lunches each day.

I have seen the father in Boston learning computer skills to get a better job so he can buy his family their first home.

I have heard the mother in Idaho welcome her son back when he was released from prison and watched her cry as she hugged her rehabilitated son.

I have watched the grandmother in Zambia holding a new water filter and grinning like she'd just been handed the world and the family in New Mexico have safe water for the first time.

I have spent days with the doctor who saw too many children die and decided "no one should have to die waiting for health care" so he created a rapid health care system for sub-Saharan African communities.

And I have watched the entrepreneur design and build a solar-powered refrigeration unit so fishermen in the same village he grew up in could prevent their catch from spoiling, enabling them to earn a good living and feed their families.

Every single one of these people helping others was just an ordinary person—someone's child, someone's parent, someone's friend.

And I noticed a pattern. So many of the founders of these organizations had come to their work through personal loss or an indignity that an injustice that didn't have to exist, existed. But the difference between them and most of the world wasn't that they had hope—it was that they refused to let hope sit still. Instead, they harnessed it into hope for others.

These days, when people ask me what matters most, I tell them the truth: It's not your résumé; it's not your bank account. What matters is the moment you lean down to pick someone up. The moment you open a door that changes someone's trajectory. The moment you share a story that makes another person feel less alone. The moment you allow yourself to really listen to someone.

I used to think life was about building. Now I know—it's about feeling life; listening intently to the sounds around us, the voices that too often are not heard; seeing those around us as they exist; and most of all helping whenever and wherever you can. You see, two things can be true. The world can be full of flaws but also full of promise. To fulfill this promise, you must believe in what's possible and believe in the power of human beings to make a difference in the world that exists—to change things. A belief anchored in hope for a better tomorrow for others, not just ourselves. A belief not powered by anger or resentment for what has occurred, but centered on what might occur.

Hope is believing that something better is possible—and doing our part to make it real. It's our ability to imagine a future different from the present and to act toward it. This belief has cured diseases, ended injustices, and fueled technological and scientific discoveries.

The greatest advances of our time began with someone who refused to accept that things had to stay the way they were—someone who thought, *There has to be a better way.* The good news is that hope is forward looking.

The great tennis star Roger Federer put much of this into context in his commencement speech at Dartmouth College in 2024. He famously told the graduates that while he had won 80% of all his matches, he had only won 54% of all points. The statistic stunned the audience and the millions of folks who have since watched that speech. Federer's message was profoundly simple—a point is just a point. And when it's behind you, it's behind you and the next point is still ahead of you. That's what matters now.

In a world full of challenges, the last "point" is always behind you. What you do with the next one is up to you.

This book is about everyday people making that next point count. They are leaning in to the problems in front of them, searching for new solutions to address them, and diving into the hard work that ultimately makes a huge difference in the lives of others.

In the next chapters, you'll meet a few of them. Folks who have harnessed their hope into action. They are learners and leaders whose eyes and ears are open, who hear the voices too often ignored, who share the fundamental characteristic of leaders who succeed in this effort—the power to look hard beyond the status quo. They *see* instead beyond the impossible and look for what is possible.

Here's what I've learned: When you are open to it, hope will find you. It's not abstract or mystical or fleeting. It's tangible and real. It's stubborn. It refuses to go away. It grows in cracked sidewalks, in crowded hospitals, in boardrooms where someone refuses to accept "that's just the way it is."

I wrote this book to share these experiences and to bring to life for you some of the remarkable people that have opened my eyes to what's possible. These incredible "acts of hope" have made a difference in my life and the lives of millions of people around the world. Their efforts have forever changed me, and I hope their stories will do the same for you.

What I have seen, and what I know, is that hope

allows people to dream, to act, and to build something better—even when everything around them says otherwise.

Without hope, we just survive. With hope, we create.

The difference between these two states of being is not some insurmountable change; it is, simply, a matter of hope.

Chapter 1

Nana Intervenes and the World Is Never the Same

"No one, anywhere, should die waiting for health care."

—Ari Johnson, MD, CEO, Muso Health

I first met Ari Johnson in the fall of 2014. I had just started at DRK the year before and had met with a number of our entrepreneurs and leaders over the previous 12 months, but there was something profoundly different about Ari. At first it was hard to put it into words. And then we asked him to speak to a group of our donors at the Charles

Hotel in Cambridge. As Ari began to speak, it became clear what was so different about him. He was able to carry two very different powerful emotions at the same time. When he spoke, the room quieted down—not because he spoke loudly, but because he was almost whispering. His voice conveyed a profound sadness and moral outrage that the inequities in health care he was seeing on the ground in Mali existed and that the world seemed not to care. He simultaneously held the belief—almost a certainty—that he and his team would be able to fix it. At that moment, I knew what I had sensed so deeply in him; it was that he saw the world's problems as his own.

Let me introduce you to his remarkable backstory.

In early 2005, Ari was living in KwaZulu-Natal, the southeastern portion of South Africa bound to the north by Swaziland, now called Eswatini, and Mozambique. He was working as a research assistant studying the barriers that young people faced with HIV testing and treatment at ground zero of the global AIDS crisis. It was a time when approximately 40% of pregnant moms were testing positive for HIV and the first trickle of antiretroviral medications was just starting to arrive in this rural town.[1] He was learning through research—publishing academic papers, writing book chapters, and giving conference presentations—about what those barriers were and why folks weren't getting the testing and treatment they needed. And he felt his work wasn't helping anybody. His neighbors all around him were still dying.

Everywhere he looked, cruelty seemed more contagious than hope.

He became frustrated and disillusioned by the path of pure research, realizing that he couldn't just watch and simply bear witness without action. There had to be more that he could do. He told me he needed to do something that mattered.

In June 2005, just around his twenty-third birthday, the opportunity to make a difference on the ground presented itself in the peri-urban communities of Yirimadio, on the edge of Mali's capital, Bamako, and he has never been the same since.

One of his mentors, Professor Patricia Symonds, had connected him with a group of young Malians

1 Ayesha BM Kharsany et al., "Trends in HIV Prevalence in Pregnant Women in Rural South Africa," *Journal of Acquired Immune Deficiency Syndromes* 10, no. 3 (2015): 289–95, DOI: 10.1097/QAI.0000000000000761.

and Americans who shared the same concerns about unequal access to health care in Mali.

When he landed in the capital of Mali in early June, it was 100 degrees and humid. It was the early rainy season—"the mango rains," as they are called, because these powerful storms knock the mangoes out of trees.

He spent the first night in a small apartment in the community. The proximity was critical to their work. They wanted to understand firsthand the connection between extreme poverty and health. And then something completely unexpected happened. Nana Niaré entered his life.

Nana was 56 years old, a retired nurse, and a matriarch in the Yirimadio communities where Muso Health's cofounders hoped to serve.

Nana's family, the Niaré family, were known as the founding family of Bamako. Nana served for more than 30 years as a nurse at a community health center where she focused on maternal and child health. She played a central role in Yirimadio's development, advocating to bring clean water access to communities, leading women's groups, providing free health care services out of her home, running a neighborhood sanitation service, and supporting neighbors in crisis.

Muso Health

Nana Niaré smiles at the photographer as she sits on a bench in the Yirimadio community of Mali, Africa, in 2007.

She was strong, very strong. And determined. Her face and presence conveyed a sense of knowing well beyond her years. No one messed around with her.

At first she saw Ari as another misguided American who had come to teach her what to do. You see, the communities of Yirimadio had seen many health workers and development projects come and go, along with short-term commitments, leaving behind only broken promises.

But there was something different about Ari. She

felt his sadness for others and his sadness for what he had seen, but she also felt the depth of his heart and his seemingly endless hope for a better world. She decided to hear him out about why he had come and then she did something quite extraordinary—something Ari had never experienced in his life. She invited Ari and the other cofounders of Muso to move in with her and the communities of Yirimadio, so that her community would become theirs. She invited this group of young people into her home, her community, her family. She shared her home, for the rest of her life and beyond.

There was understandably considerable skepticism when a group of American and Malian young people arrived hoping to help. But while others responded with reasonable skepticism, Nana did something different, something transformative. In the face of the failures of many past short-term projects from outside partners, she offered a radical, long-term commitment.

Ari and three other fellow teammates moved to Yirimadio at Nana's invitation, in and near Nana's home: physician Djoume Diakite, Fulbright Scholar (and now obstetrician) Jessica Beckerman, educator Moise Samaké, and Ari.

Muso Health

Muso cofounders (left to right) Ari Johnson, Nana Niaré, and Jessica Beckerman stand side by side and smile at the photographer in the Yirimadio community of Mali, Africa, in 2016.

At first Ari couldn't believe it and for a moment he wasn't sure if he should take her up on it.

He could never imagine anyone, including himself, making that offer to a group of doctors visiting him in San Francisco. Imagining the best version of himself, he could see himself offering to cook them dinner, take them to see patients, but never to invite strangers into his home to live with him permanently.

But there was something about Nana that was profoundly different, and though he had no idea how important her offer was at the time, he later learned that the very act of moving in with her would change his life and his work forever.

At the time, one in seven kids in Nana's community were dying before the children made it to kindergarten. They had seen, as Ari put it, "an entire graveyard of broken promises." Their families would travel from other areas to go to Nana's house to talk. And she would listen to them. She didn't have a lot of resources, but she would do whatever she could to help. And because she had invited Ari to live with her and be near her, he learned how he could really help.

When folks came to see her, she would put her hand on the couch and say to Ari, "Come sit with me. Let's listen to our neighbor here."

She wouldn't push. She wouldn't dictate what Ari and the team should do from there. She led Ari to learn that the first part of helping someone is to listen to them, to sit with them, to truly hear them.

He learned from Nana what no textbook or conference could teach. That real change begins with listening.

Mothers sat and told their stories of childhood and family ailments. These stories became the blueprint and the moment that the idea behind Muso

Health began. The moment that started everything that enabled Ari and his team to gain insights about what the future of health care could look like, which he and the team would never have come to understand otherwise. They saw a better future. The despair and frustration he felt in South Africa turned into endless hope and belief. That was the gift that Nana had given them.

And the memories of that moment have not faded with time. They remain as vivid today as they did then. As Ari told me and as he described in detail in the podcast episode "More Than Enough" with Kate Bowler, here's how it happened.[2]

A grandmother came to see Nana and asked if she would go see her grandson, Ibraham. Ari knew it was serious and so they quickly made their way to her house. Her grandson was soaked in sweat from a high fever, and was having trouble breathing. Although they rushed him to the nearest hospital, they were too late.

So, the next day, Ari and the team were sitting at Ibraham's funeral, still processing the death of this baby. The trauma of watching this child's family watch him die and knowing similar events were

2 Kate Bowler, host, "More Than Enough," *Everything Happens with Kate Bowler*, season 4, episode 6, March 12, 2019, podcast, 31 min., www.katebowler.com/podcasts/ari-johnson-more-than-enough/.

happening every day changed Ari, and changed the course of his life. Because the sadness of knowing these deaths could have been prevented was nearly unbearable. But, over time, something unexpected happened. The community began to trust Ari and his team and each day more and more people were waiting outside for help. While they were still having difficulty finding health care in a system that had excluded them, they no longer were helpless. Because they now had Ari and the team to help them through this. And the team did just that.

And soon, they learned the most important lesson—that time was the problem. When they could help families in the community find access to health care quickly, the outcomes were different.

By accompanying hundreds of patients one by one, and through their research, Ari and the team learned from patients about the barriers they faced—the reason they couldn't get care in time, fees they couldn't afford to pay, distances they couldn't afford to travel, providers without the skills or the equipment they needed to make the diagnosis and provide a cure. What Nana's neighbors taught them was what a different kind of health care system could look like. One that worked closely with community and government partners to establish a network of community health workers.

And Nana knew what the team had just discovered—something all the teams that had come before to help had failed to see. The real insight was they were trying to fix the wrong problem. The problem wasn't a disease-specific problem, or the cost of medicine, or the equity of access to care, or the need for transportation to get care, or the need for adequate facilities to treat illness, or the need for trained caregivers to provide care. It was actually all of those things that contributed to the real problem that was hidden behind each of those constraints: delay of care.

Fixing any one of the individual constraints would never fix the entirety of the problem or reduce mortality. It would just fix that one part of the problem, which would only lead to the next constraint that delayed care. But by identifying each of the binding constraints and the sequence to follow and fix each one of them, Ari and the Muso team had a specific road map to follow that could solve the underlying cause of disease and mortality.

Together with community partners, they needed to design and build a different kind of health care system, to remove structural barriers by meeting patients where they are.

So they created Muso Health to do just that.

They recruited, trained, equipped, and hired local community health workers to take the lead, bringing diagnostic testing and medicine door-to-door. The team renovated the local government clinic and expanded the primary care team. Care became available free of charge, with no co-pays.

Medicine became accessible. Fees were removed and care was provided free with equitable distribution. Transportation to care was given to improve facilities where care could be dispensed. And, even better, the solution could be applied to different geographies with similar results. And the results spoke for themselves.

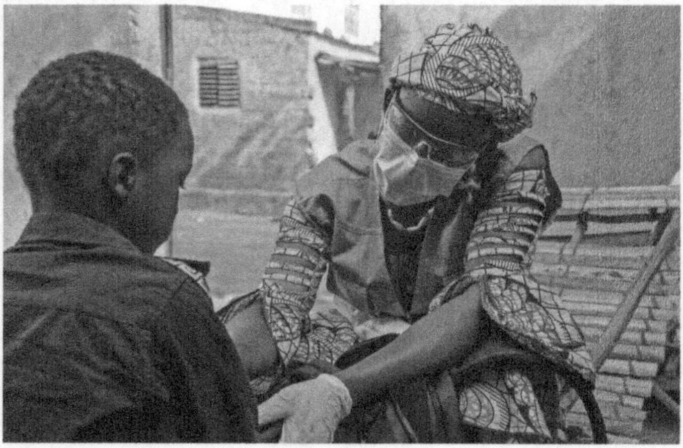

Muso Health

Professional community health worker Aissata Coulibaly provides care to a young boy during routine home visits in the Yirimadio community of Mali, Africa, in March 2021.

This was what Nana had predicted when she first welcomed the team, saying, "If you live with us and listen to us, there will be no end to how much good you can do." And she was right. And the results were amazing. Ari continued to explain on the "More Than Enough" podcast episode with Kate Bowler that "just a few dollars' worth of pills would cure a child from malaria or from a pneumonia infection. A few dollars' worth of care, a little bit of effort, was enough to completely turn their life around. That little bit of effort, and you see this Lazarus-like effect."[3]

Muso has established the standard of care for communities across Mali, providing care to hundreds of thousands of people. As a result, the communities of Yirimadio now have the lowest child mortality rates in sub-Saharan Africa. It went from one of the highest child mortality rates to the lowest rate in less than a decade, achieved by truly understanding the full landscape of the problem and unpacking the contributory factors.

Nana passed in 2020 at the age of 70, but she made sure her home remained Ari's home and her family, his family.

---

3 Bowler, "More Than Enough," *Everything Happens with Kate Bowler.*

Muso Health

Salimata Samaké in the Yirimadio community of Mali, Africa, looks down at her arm as a professional community health worker measures it using a mid-upper-arm circumference (MUAC) tape to assess for malnutrition.

Nana's gift of hope endures in a team of more than 1,000 people, in more than 20 million patient visits to date—moments to walk beside a neighbor, listen to what really matters to them, and commit to care.

Hope, Ari learned, isn't passive. It's not waiting for the rain to end; rather, it's uncovering simple acts of humanity and kindness within the storm.

It's something I have seen over and over again in my own life.

Muso Health

Dr. Noumoutié Sanogo, capacity building manager for community health centers and associations, smiles for the camera while standing in front of the Diapé Primary Care Center in the Adzopé district of Côte d'Ivoire, alongside three members of the health center staff in November 2022.

Chapter 2

Build the Biggest Tent You Can

"When we push, the world moves."

—Clementine Jacoby, CEO, Recidiviz

It was early 2018 when I first met Clem. She had just arrived at our San Francisco office, and as she sat down in our conference room there was an energy about her that was impossible to ignore. She had just left Google to start Recidiviz, a criminal justice data platform, and she was thinking deeply about how change happens in the world.

She had just flown to see her dad, Wade Jacoby, who was one of the most recognized comparative political economists. His research focused on complex societies and how informal coalitions could be created among diverse groups to create lasting policy reform, notably Germany and the European Union's expansion to Eastern Europe.

For an academic, Wade was known for his deep embrace of relationships and in particular his drive to include as many voices in his thinking and in his world as possible, regardless of whether they agreed with his views or not. He had come to believe that lasting change only occurs when a diverse group of individuals build consensus on an issue. And the way to do that is to build a big tent that can house all these different perspectives.

Clem was clearly a rising social entrepreneur. Everybody who met her had no doubt that she had the capability to create something significant. She was focused on understanding how people get stuck in our criminal justice system. Like one in five Americans, she had a personal connection to the question. Her uncle had been sentenced to 10 years in prison for a nonviolent offense at 19. Decades later, he was still in prison, caught in the revolving door of incarceration that so many young men enter and never exit.

Clem discovered that her uncle's journey—trying to follow what felt like a narrow and invisible path home—was not unique. She learned that in America, home of the free, we incarcerate more people for longer than any other country—in part because so many people enter young and never really come home. In fact, 20% of individuals released from prison are re-incarcerated within the first year, and those on probation and parole constitute nearly half of all prison admissions in the United States. This led her to think about all the other "uncles" who were caught in the system as well.

Clementine Jacoby

Wade and Clementine Jacoby in 1997, the year Clementine's uncle was sentenced to prison.

Clem and a small group of her fellow software engineers set out to understand how this could be possible. They built the first version of Recidiviz to explore public sources of criminal justice data, creating open-source tools for researchers and advocates, thinking transparency might help interrupt the cycles of recidivism.

That was until they were connected to Leann Bertsch, who led the North Dakota Department of Corrections and Rehabilitation. Leann told them that while it was great they were excited about the issue, they were solving the wrong problem. Her team wasn't withholding data from the outside world; they were struggling to access it themselves. Leann was clear: If you want to understand the problem, just come to Bismarck.

That's how Clem and her team—two other volunteers—ended up in Bismarck, North Dakota.

Leann had cracked the door open for Recidiviz. She'd offered them the chance to get to know the problem from the inside.

They were stunned by what they saw. Offices with shelves lined with thousands of paper files. Staff juggling dozens of log-ins to systems that didn't speak to each other. Lists of reentry resources filled with long-disconnected phone numbers. Parole officers with caseloads so large they didn't have a chance to help any one individual succeed. Decision-makers without the data to see what programs were working.

The team shadowed as many of Leann's staff as

they could, trying to map out where information was falling through the cracks. Every day revealed a new gap—data fields that didn't match across systems, eligibility rules buried in policy manuals, processes that relied on paper forms or memory.

They watched one parole officer try to determine whether a client was eligible for release. She toggled between five different databases, each with separate log-ins and authentication protocols.

She said most of her time went to five people on her caseload who were really struggling, which meant that the other ninety-five people she worked with were sort of in a holding pattern—including maybe twenty who shouldn't have been on supervision at all and another forty who were one piece of paperwork away from release.

This enormous system, responsible for the lives of millions of Americans, was run on a constellation of disconnected databases and creaking software. The underlying fragmentation made it hard to know who was eligible for anything—including who had already earned their release from prison—and what they might need to actually succeed, and stay out. The problem was a big one, and solving it wouldn't be easy. But Clem's father's advice kept playing in her head. "If you want to really support change in a country that you care about, you have to be willing to pay the price of long-term engagement. Democracies can't be sustained with short-term thinking. They just can't be."

Solving this problem for the long term would require building a big tent that had lots of people with different ideas and then working really hard to find thin threads of alignment that everyone could agree on, even if they might disagree about everything else.

The problems plaguing corrections data seemed to be one of those rare issues, like her dad had described, that everyone could agree on.

No one was happy with how the system was working. Not the people locked up, who were in the dark about release dates and what "time" they were earning and losing through layered and overlapping policies. Not the advocates, who had worked hard to pass those policies that weren't being fully implemented. Not Leann's staff, who showed up every day wanting to help people, but didn't have the tools or the time. Not Leann, who was tasked with safely housing a rising population on a tightening budget. Nobody liked that people were getting stuck because of scattered data.

Once they identified it, agreeing on the problem turned out to be surprisingly easy. But solving the problems that plagued corrections data would be much harder.

So Clem left Bismarck with a new vision for Recidiviz. The system's tools needed to be overhauled. And they would start with tools specifically for the leaders and staff running corrections agencies. Designing enterprise-grade software for corrections was far from what they expected to be working on, but it would become the foundation of their big tent.

Recidiviz started building tools that closed those information gaps.

They built prototypes that automated case managers' most repetitive tasks: identifying people who were eligible for release, filling out the right forms, finding and connecting people to the right rehabilitative opportunities, and helping officers prioritize their caseloads. The goal wasn't to replace staff—it was to free them up to do the social work that actually makes a difference.

They started expanding to more states—red, blue, big, small. Large, complex ones like Texas and California. Nimble, aggressive ones like Utah and Maine. States with different underlying beliefs about crime and punishment, but a shared desire for change—to rein in ballooning costs, to ensure that the rules on their books were actually being applied, to address the grueling toll on underpaid and overworked staff.

States where staff were using Recidiviz's early tools began to see tangible results. They cut the time that people spent waiting for opportunities they were already eligible for by 24%. They saw a 15% increase in people moving through those opportunities—out of solitary confinement, from prison to work release, from parole to freedom, and more. They saw recidivism drop by 16%.

Those results built trust, and the opportunity to tackle the challenge from new angles. Massachusetts was the first state to ask Recidiviz to build tools for its prison population, sharing information about each person's sentence and how to earn time off through good behavior and programming. Empowering them with this information saved even more time for staff, who spend a good chunk of their day responding to repetitive requests. More importantly, it engaged the people with the most at stake in their own rehabilitation, shining a light on the pathway home.

Utah was the first state to think beyond their own agency walls, exploring how to expand their new case planning infrastructure to law enforcement and other agencies working with the same vulnerable populations. They are predicting that intervening with the right tools sooner might help some people avoid prison in the first place.

And to be clear, there were no shortcuts. Engaging more stakeholders doesn't result in the fastest rollouts or simplest solutions; there are more user journeys to map and more questions about accuracy and access. But it does get more people pushing in the same direction and builds longer-lasting change. Again, the big tent is what it's all about.

Recidiviz

Clementine Jacoby with corrections leaders from Rhode Island and Indiana in 2025.

The solutions Recidiviz built needed to be resilient. Things change quickly in the world, and opinions can change fast. In only 20 years, from 1980 to 2000, America saw its prison population quadruple, resulting in social and economic consequences we are still grappling with today. Children who have a parent who has been to prison—that is, 7% of American children—are 3 times as likely to go to prison themselves and twice as likely to be homeless. American families with loved ones in prison lose $350 billion every year in direct costs and lost earnings. While there remains fierce debate about how to solve so many parts of these problems, one thing everyone can agree on is that data should inform the discussion, not hold people back.

Today, Recidiviz tools have helped accelerate the release of 250,000 people from the criminal justice system in 19 states, covering about half (46%) of the US prison population. That's thousands of mothers who have their sons and daughters back, thousands of siblings who have their brothers and sisters back, and thousands of children who have their parents back.

The team is now more than 100 people, each drawn to the work for different reasons.

In other words, the big tent works.

Sadly, Wade Jacoby passed away unexpectedly in 2020. But Recidiviz remains a testament to his conviction. Build the biggest tent you can. Bring everyone in. If it works here, it can work anywhere. And the advice he passed on to Clem lives on in the big tent that she built.

She built the biggest tent she could build, never let perfection be the enemy of good, and never ever gave up hope and belief there was a path forward that would change the destiny of those who needed help.

Wade's words and life shaped much of Clem's early thinking about the world and how to create lasting change. His lessons became the foundation upon which she built her "big tent," one wide enough to hold hope, perseverance, and imperfect progress.

Recidiviz

Clementine, Recidiviz team members, and corrections leaders from across the country at the 2025 Recidiviz Partner Summit.

We are all creatures of those who have invested in our lives.

And like Clem, I, too, am a product of those who invested deeply in me, as my parents instilled in me from an early age the conviction that giving back is not a choice but a way of life. They lived that belief daily with generosity, with curiosity, and with an unshakable joy for the world and all it offers.

I may have taken their zest for life a bit too literally in my first three decades (to their mild dismay), but through every twist and turn, their guidance was a steady hand.

Though they have been gone for more than a decade, the way they lived continues to shape me—just as I hope, in time, some part of me will live on in my daughter, my son-in-law, and their children.

Jim Bildner

Rob, Allen, and Jim Bildner in Montauk, New York.

Chapter 3

Compelled to Make a Difference in the World

"We can't fix all the problems in the world, but we can fix this one."

—Kiah Williams, cofounder, SIRUM

While people see problems in the world all the time, few feel compelled to change them and even fewer can imagine how that change can take place. Kiah Williams is an exception. I have never met a more tenacious fighter for good.

When I first met Kiah in the fall of 2013, she and her SIRUM cofounders, Adam Kircher and George Wang, were working out of shared office space in the public service center at Stanford, where they had all been students. They had decided to try solving the shortage of affordable prescription medicine available to vulnerable populations who desperately needed them. Further complicating this problem was the fact that there was an excess of these very same drugs that had been prescribed and dispensed to patients in health care facilities that, when the patient got discharged, had to be literally incinerated or otherwise disposed of. When they first saw this happening, it seemed like it must be an anomaly, but they soon discovered it was the rule and was happening everywhere.

This was not just an isolated problem; the supply/demand imbalance was embedded in the business model of the pharmaceutical supply chain and in the country's provision of health care. No one seemed to be vested in solving for it.

Anyone looking at this team of three against the size of the problem they were trying to solve would give them low odds of even making a dent. Plus, they had few resources at their disposal. To say their startup office was lean would be an understatement. And as Kiah would say time and time again in later years, they were naive in so many ways about what it would take to change this inequity. But it was that naivete and their unrelenting tenacity to not let this blatant inequity stand that powered them through the early years and seasoned their entrepreneurial skills quickly.

They became experts, fast.

SIRUM

George Wang, Kiah Williams, and Adam Kircher, cofounders of SIRUM.

What they learned is that 50 million people have difficulty affording their medications because prescription costs are too high. At the same time, the amount of prescription medications being wasted is unimaginable—about $11 billion of unused medicine goes to waste every year because the patient it was prescribed for no longer needs it or because of surplus in the supply chain. Virtually all of that waste is destroyed and thrown out, amounting to 10,000 tons of medication waste annually. And yet more people die each year from not taking their medicine than from opioid overdoses and car accidents combined. The few who had recognized the issue felt helpless to do anything about it. Even the nurses in health care facilities who saw this dichotomy every day, and who initially were outraged by it, became immune to it over time.

But for the SIRUM team, it was simply outrageous that this could be happening, and it deeply resonated with what the founders had seen in their own lives. Adam had seen from afar the devastation that the tsunami in Indonesia had created in communities and watched how desperately needed medicine and supplies were going to waste because on-the-ground relief workers couldn't get them to where they were needed.

Kiah had seen a similar problem firsthand when she was a health coach in Oakland with patients who were trying to get better and do the things they needed to do, but like the island communities in Indonesia, they simply couldn't get the medicine they needed—something she saw happening over and over again.

The fact that 10 million low-income adults with chronic illnesses who are uninsured or underinsured cannot afford the medicine they need; that one-third of uninsured adults have said they stopped taking medications as prescribed because of cost; that even with insurance, half of the people earning less than

$35,000 a year do not fill prescriptions if their insurance cannot cover them; and that, at the very same time, billions of dollars of perfectly good prescriptions were being literally destroyed while millions of people couldn't get access to these very same drugs was just flat out unacceptable.

Kiah, Adam, and George began to imagine a different world where the supply/demand imbalance could be fixed.

That's lesson one: When confronted with the seemingly impossible, let your imagination see a different construct.

Lesson two: Act on it.

The world they imagined was a world where there was a Match.com-like platform for medicine that would allow donors to easily upload prescription surpluses, instead of throwing them away, and allow recipients who needed medication to get it. The platform they imagined would then connect donor and recipient organizations and coordinate donation logistics including itemized drug manifests, tracking, and shipping. One of their biggest insights was that they could prove the efficacy of this strategy without an expensive and time-consuming technology buildout. They could prove the pilot with five things: cardboard boxes, a pair of scissors, packing tape, FedEx labels, and permission to send the drugs from the donor to the receiving community health center, clinic, or pharmacy.

And that's exactly what they set about to do.

The task? Make it as easy to donate the unused medicine as it was to throw them away. So, if you were a nursing home, hospital, pharmacy, or wholesaler, all you had to do was put a SIRUM-provided recycling bin in your facility. When the box filled up, the health center let SIRUM know, and then SIRUM handled all of the logistics and paperwork needed to get that medication to where it was most needed.

For the end recipient, it was game changing.

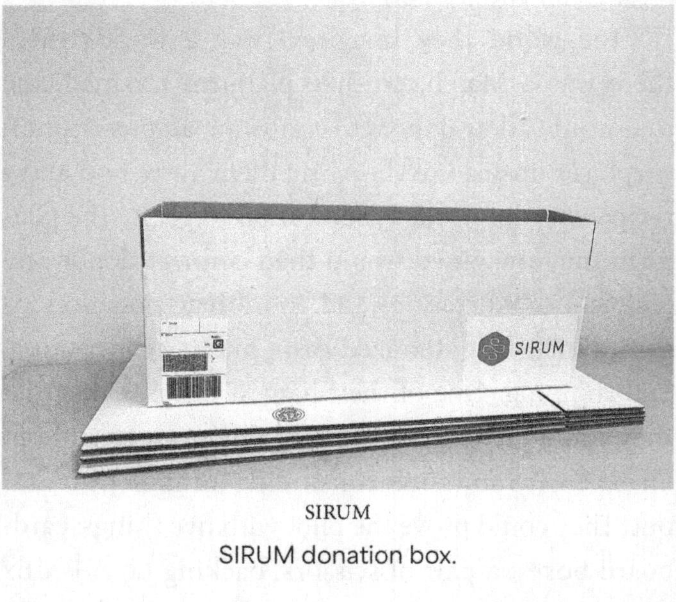

SIRUM

SIRUM donation box.

Take a patient we'll call Monika as an example. A mom with twins, she has high blood pressure and is trying to do everything right to take care of her family, but money is tight. So, she called multiple pharmacies to try to find better prices for the meds she needed. While there were multiple sources for the prescription, she still couldn't afford them until Kiah and her team connected her to Good Pill, the home delivery pharmacy that SIRUM had launched and powered with donated medications.[4] Good Pill mails affordable prescriptions directly to people's homes, most for only $2/month.

And Monika is not alone. There are so many other "Monika"s who are trying to take care of their health, who are going above and beyond to try to do the right thing for themselves and their families, but who the system has failed. They shouldn't have to call around to six, seven, eight, nine pharmacies to find an affordable price for blood pressure medication they need so they can be there for their family.

What drove Kiah to do all this? Kiah saw these systemic disparities growing up. It was all too familiar. She grew up in a lower-income community in West Philly and straddled two worlds. She attended the same public magnet school that the mayor's son

---

4 Good Pill, www.goodpill.org.

went to. But unlike the mayor's son, for Kiah to get to school, she had to traverse multiple neighborhoods, including some of the most marginalized across Philly. Every day the commute entailed a one-hour-and-twenty-minute trip that required walking to the bus, taking the bus to the train, transferring to another train, and then making a four-block walk to school. She was struck by what she saw—how different worlds existed at the same time in her own community, sometimes just blocks apart from each other. Some communities had no doctors and residents had to travel an hour to get to one. In the next community, you could see one of the leading doctors in the world. She commuted through neighborhoods where there were no grocery stores yet she saw other neighborhoods with an abundance of stores.

Kiah had to have a very wide aperture—seeing how different life could be and being able to straddle both worlds every day as she went to school in one world and returned home to another.

When she got older, she started recognizing these differences as disparities. And in college, she looked deeper at the systems and saw the inconsistencies, and her conclusion was that these disparities shouldn't exist.

At the same time, she was constantly aware of the privileges she had received in her own life.

Her father grew up in a one-room apartment and worked his way to get to college and law school and provide for Kiah and her brother so they could get a good education and be able to pursue their dreams.

Kiah learned early on that too many people don't get to choose what's in their life; the world chooses it for them. It's constantly putting hard choices in front of them, making them decide whether they can buy the prescriptions they need, or defer so they can pay rent or buy food. For Kiah, not only was this inherently unfair; it was intolerable.

Attending the magnet school, she felt like she won the lottery. She was determined to become the first doctor in the family. She understood that her privilege came from the blood, sweat, and tears of her father and quickly developed the belief that *If I can get a better life, then others should be able to get it too.*

Kiah felt compelled to make a difference in the lives of others.

She thought hope was a luxury she couldn't afford. What she learned later, and as others have said in previous chapters, is that a large part of hope is taking action to bring to reality a different world.

Kiah did get accepted to medical school. But she deferred three times to start SIRUM and never looked back. She had a much more important mission in front of her. One of her cofounders, Adam, took a leave of absence from Harvard Business School (HBS) to work on SIRUM. He never went back. They had found a better purpose—saving medicine to save lives.

Kiah Williams

Kiah visits her old high school in Philly.

Kiah, George, and Adam's outrage and persistence turned their imagination into a reality. SIRUM's systems and infrastructure have created the nation's largest medicine redistribution platform. They not only redistribute much-needed prescriptions, but they also have developed technological systems that help community health providers manage their inventory of donated medicine so they know what they can offer to patients in need.

SIRUM has grown to a platform and a program that redistributes prescription medicine across 11 states—getting more than $300 million of medicine to 700,000 people—and continues growing exponentially.

SIRUM

Donated medications ready to be redistributed to patients.

SIRUM demonstrates that the actions of one person can change the destiny of hundreds and thousands and millions.

After all, it's a matter of hope and a belief that a different world can exist.

Chapter 4

Your Destiny Is in Your Hands to Create

"There is hope in the unseen."

—Aimée Eubanks Davis, CEO, Braven

I first talked with Aimée in the spring of 2016. She had just finished a tough meeting with one of our managing directors and a group of experts at the HBS office.

Aimée was nervous going into the meeting despite her incredible résumé and her prior senior experience at Teach For America. The assembled group at HBS were known for their candid and straightforward feedback, and Aimée was in the early stages of thinking about and bringing to reality a new organization focused on solving the inequity of educational attainment in the United States. True to form, the group had a lot of feedback for her. It was tough hearing all the things they thought needed to be addressed in Aimée's model, particularly when she was so early in her thinking. The managing director who was with Aimée at the meeting called me and asked me to talk to Aimée. I gave her a call to ask her how she was doing after the meeting. When she picked up the phone, she heard my voice and laughed. "I expected your call. Listen, Jim, if I can't handle that kind of feedback, I am in deep trouble. For my whole life I've had to handle folks who questioned what I was trying to do, and have learned that in everything said, there is always some truth. The key is to be open to it and use it to make your idea better. They made some good points in that meeting and I am thinking about how I can apply them in real time as we speak," she said.

That three-minute conversation encapsulates Aimée's secret sauce—she is always listening and always learning, despite having already achieved so much. It's a lesson we can all take to heart.

Here is how her journey started.

Aimée was two, being held in someone's arms and looking down at her father's casket.

Even today, she remembers the brown velveteen dress she was wearing, the white ribbons in her hair, a room filled with sadness, and the sight of her father's lifeless body.

Her father, Larry, had passed away from leukemia, a disease he had suffered from since Aimée was nine months old.

Aimée's understanding of her father is shaped by others' stories—how he was incredibly hardworking and generous, and how much he doted on her and her sister, Rebekah.

But she saw the impact of his passing firsthand. It changed her family's path instantly and completely. Her mother, Sharon, became a single mom of two young girls overnight, saddled with debt from dental school, which Larry was just six months away from completing. She suddenly had to find a new way of living and operating.

As with others you have read about in this book, despair at this moment was close at hand. What Aimée saw was her mother shaking off the despair and embracing the life she now had, knowing the life she had experienced before Larry died was never coming back and that the new life she could have was hers to create.

She enrolled in business classes at Governors State University, where she'd drop Rebekah and Aimée at a nursery school and head off to class, believing that education was the key to getting ahead. There she met her new husband, with whom she partnered to

Aimée Eubanks Davis

Sharon Eubanks-Pope, Larry Eubanks, Rebekah Eubanks, and Aimée at age one.

start a business together. And from that point, Aimée and her mother and sister began a journey to economic mobility.

Throughout the journey, Aimée's mom held two things close to her heart: realism about what it would take and endless hope that they would get there. Her mantra was short and sweet—*Life is going to be a challenge, but we are going to be OK*—acknowledging that life will always throw you curves, but you *can* survive them.

Aimée Eubanks Davis

Aimée, Sharon Eubanks-Pope, and Rebekah Eubanks.

Aimée's mom didn't just talk about hope; she lived it. Her mother studied late into the night after putting her children to bed, advocated for her community with steady courage, and built a stable, prosperous future for her family in the wake of profound grief and financial hardship. Those moments planted in Aimée the understanding that hope is not passive—it's the fuel for resilience, for purpose, and for creating change.

When Aimée was in high school, her mother saw that the Black students in their district, including Aimée and Rebekah, weren't always being given equal opportunities, especially to access honors classes. She came together with other Black families who'd seen their children denied opportunities at school and created a group called Parents for Parity in Education. Together, they filed a formal complaint against the district. The district investigated and found evidence of segregation in their elementary and middle schools, and placed those schools on probation for five years.

Aimée's mom saw education as the ticket to freedom, something Aimée experienced firsthand, and Aimée committed to pay it forward and help others achieve it as well.

She joined Teach For America after college and began working on Teach For America's staff a few years later. She noticed that while educators, students, and families were working incredibly hard to get students into college, only 30% of the 1.4 million students with limited financial resources or who were the first in their family to enroll in college each year actually graduated and secured a strong first job or entered graduate school. That's nearly one million students every single year who start on the path to greater economic mobility but stop short of the last step.

Aimée founded Braven to fix this last step. It empowers college students to succeed in college and secure strong first jobs.

Braven partners with higher education institutions and employers to provide students with networks, internships, and job opportunities. Braven has reached nearly 14,000 students (called "Fellows") across seven states; 94% are graduating from college, and 74% are already outearning their parents in their first job out of college.

They developed a credit-bearing college course that teaches career readiness and professional skills and continues to provide mentorship, resources, and support to Fellows for six months after they graduate.

Gian Icatar

A cohort of Fellows and their leadership coach at the Braven Learning Lab during Braven's Capstone Challenge event.

Aimée credits much of Braven's success to her mother's example and her ability to imagine a future that doesn't yet exist. She learned from her that hope is alive even when it's hope in what's not yet visible—in the possibilities, the potential, and the belief that something good will emerge. That's the belief her mom embraced when her father died.

The same hope that carried Sharon through loss and uncertainty now runs through everything Aimée does. It's the kind of hope that doesn't wait for the world to change, but helps set that change in motion.

Like her mom, Aimée is showing thousands of students that, although there will be challenges along the way, they *will* be okay.

That's what hope is all about. Not wishful thinking, as Jane Goodall famously said, but there for the making.

Braven

The Braven community.

Chapter 5

Nothing Is Impossible, Unless You Fail to See Something Different

> *"Every opportunity I ever had in life was because of education."*
>
> —Evan Marwell, founder, EducationSuperHighway

As Clem showed us with Recidiviz in chapter 2, data often is the ticket to making real change happen. It's a lesson that Evan Marwell, the founder of one of the DRK Foundation's portfolio organizations, EducationSuperHighway (ESH), knows all too well, having used data to change minds and actions over and over again in his life.

My favorite Evan story is when, in 1988, as a junior consultant with Corporate Decisions, he was asked by a partner of the firm to make a presentation of the firm's findings to the CEO and senior team of one of their clients. As a newly minted college graduate, Evan was petrified at the thought of making the presentation and asked the partner why anyone in the room would listen to anything a 23-year-old would have to say. The partner's response was quick and clear. "Evan," he said, "because you have the data. Everyone else in the room only has their opinions. Never forget, Evan, that the person in the room with the data always wins over time. Without it, you are just another voice in a room. With it, you are *the* voice."

Evan Marwell

Evan Marwell speaks to the audience at the ASU+GSV Summit.

More than almost anyone else I know, Evan has taken this lesson to heart. His work at ESH was no exception. Between 2012 and 2020, Evan and ESH used data to help 50 million students connect to broadband when no one believed there was even a problem. Here's the backstory of how that happened.

It was 2012, and Evan's life was pretty predictable.

He was a partner at a hedge fund he had started and he and his partners had raised more than $1.4 billion by 2009.

The hedge fund was successful, but by 2010, he was feeling unfulfilled. It had all started feeling very repetitive to him. They were making deals and moving money, but was it really what he was meant to do?

He quickly realized the answer was no and so in 2010 he left the hedge fund and began casting about not really knowing what to do next, but looking for something that could fulfill his need to have a job that had a purpose—something that mattered in the world and that could make a difference in the lives of others, ideally in education. Evan had grown up in a family of educators and saw firsthand, as Aimée had seen from her mom, that education was the key stepping stone to opportunity for everyone. Without it, you were at a disadvantage from the start.

By chance, he started reading a book by Felix

Rohatyn, *Bold Endeavors,* about incredible infrastructure projects that individuals made happen. It made him even more restless.

There was noise everywhere at that time in Silicon Valley about the ability of technology and the internet to change the way education was delivered, but not much to show for it.

Khan Academy had just introduced its first internet-based videos on math and people were intrigued.

And then two things happened nearly at the same time. Evan had just signed up for a stint as finance chair for the board of directors at his fifth-grade daughter's school. He became very involved with the school's finances and infrastructure. He quickly learned that her school had only one cable modem for 500 people.

They had lots of computers, but the Wi-Fi network was eight years old, couldn't reach every classroom, and was painfully slow. One student described the internet access "like sucking peanut butter through a straw."

Evan kept hearing one particular story from teachers and students.

The teachers gave an assignment, asking the students to get a laptop out of the laptop cart, pick a subject to research, watch a video about it, and then make a PowerPoint presentation to share what they learned with the rest of the class. Instantly, the problem became clear.

The technology worked for the first 10 students, but then things went south fast. By the time they got to the eleventh student, the internet basically ground to a halt and nobody could watch their videos anymore.

Evan realized the issue wasn't outdated computers; it was broadband.

The school simply didn't have enough speed.

The school wanted to buy 40 more computers and 10 laptops, and they thought that would solve the problem. Evan asked, "What about the internet?"

They looked at him with a blank stare, as if to say, "What do you mean?"

It occurred to him that if the private school his daughter was attending didn't have adequate internet speed, public schools with less funding must have a similar or worse issue.

All of a sudden, he was consumed with solving this problem but wasn't sure where to start.

And then, as luck would have it, he got invited to attend a meeting at the White House with other tech leaders to help the administration think about the role of technology in driving the American economy and making technology more accessible. He was flattered at first, but didn't think he would have much to say. He then remembered the problem that his daughter's school was having.

At the meeting, President Obama went around the room and asked each guest what they thought was the biggest technology challenge the country faced. Person after person cited the usual challenges—manufacturing, government's lack of technology competence, regulation, etc. Then it was Evan's turn. He said, "We have an internet issue in our schools." Everyone turned to look at him and he repeated it. "Look," he said, "my daughter goes to a private school in San Francisco that can afford almost anything they need, but they have lousy internet speed. I researched the problem and realized it's true across the board. We need to go fix broadband and internet access at schools across the country, and do it now before it really impacts the delivery of education in our schools."

Evan told them he found a survey that indicated more than 70% of schools had insufficient internet speed. He repeated his plea: "You guys need to fix it."

The first chief technology officer of the United States at the time, Aneesh Chopra, who organized the meeting, sat down next to Evan and said, "You should fix that problem."

Evan was stunned.

He turned to Chopra and said, "Sir, that's your job." But Chopra told Evan that it's actually a problem they can't fix. That government isn't set up to do it. He said, "We can call attention to it but, Evan, you are the one who needs to fix it." He explained to Evan that a federal program already existed, called E-Rate. It spent $2.4 billion a year to put broadband in schools, and 99% of the country's schools had broadband.

Evan told him, "Well, that might be true, but all the schools have cable modems and very slow Wi-Fi networks, which makes learning impossible. The E-Rate program may exist, but it's not solving the problem."

And then Evan remembered the book *Bold Endeavors*. In each chapter, one individual took on a massive problem and stayed with it until they finally got the government to put up the money to support the efforts.

Evan had found his purpose. He was going to equip every school in America with high-speed internet, connecting 50 million kids to the technology they deserved regardless of how rich or poor their school systems were.

He set up a new organization, EducationSuperHighway, and soon hired a team to take on this challenge. And as they soon discovered, there were a number of them.

The first was convincing the Federal Communications Commission (FCC) to modernize the E-Rate program for the twenty-first century. At one point, he managed to get a call with the FCC's chief of staff, who politely listened to Evan's pitch about why and how the program needed to change and who then asked, "Where are we going to get the money to pay for the fiber schools need?"

Evan's response: "Stop spending $600 million per year on phone service for schools. No one uses dial-up internet anymore."

The chief of staff was incredulous. "We are not spending $600 million on phone service." And then he hung up on Evan. Three weeks later, he called back and said, "I told you we weren't spending $600 million on phone service—it's actually $650 million!"

That one piece of data changed everything, and from then on Evan became the FCC's most important partner in modernizing the E-Rate program, which ultimately enabled schools to install the fiber they needed.

Later, Evan had to figure out how to get schools

to work with him. He had convinced the US Department of Education to work with him, but it turned out they didn't actually talk to schools.

It was his mother who came to the rescue.

When she was in the supermarket one day, she ran into an old boss who was running technology for the Wisconsin Department of Public Instruction. She told him what Evan was trying to do and he said, "We know we need better internet in our schools and we can help him connect with the right people." Six weeks later, Evan and his team were in contact with 70% of the schools in Wisconsin, and they started taking the same approach in other states.

Fast-forward to 2019. Evan gathered data through speed tests to prove the problem existed, then he leveraged the data to build widespread commitment from key stakeholders, partnered with the government, and provided implementation support. They partnered with governors in all 50 states to drive upgrades and provided technical and procurement support to school districts, enabling these states to connect 99% of schools across the country while using data to create transparency about what schools should pay for broadband, reducing the cost of broadband by 92%.

EducationSuperHighway

Students receive broadband in schools across America thanks to EducationSuperHighway.

It wasn't easy, but he got it done.

As Rohatyn writes in *Bold Endeavors*, "One person, committed to solving a problem, who can imagine a different future, has the power to change the trajectory for millions."

Evan was that person.

EducationSuperHighway

Center: Evan Marwell, CEO of EducationSuperHighway, surrounded by students who now have access to broadband in school.

Chapter 6

The Lesson from the TV

"They were fainting and they were hungry. I just knew that I had to do something."

—Wawira Njiru, founder and CEO, Food4Education

Wawira entered my life in October 2017 when I met with her and our team in Boston. By then she already had a reputation as a force of nature. At 26 years old, she had already attracted considerable attention, and at the time of this writing, at 34, she has accumulated even more recognition, including the first-ever Global Citizen Prize: Cisco Youth Leadership Award in 2018, the United Nations

Person of the Year (Kenya) in 2021, the Icon Award (the World's 50 Best Restaurants) in 2022, the Skoll Award for Social Innovation in 2024, the Elevate Prize in 2024, the TED Audacious Project in 2024, CNBC's Changemaker (Women Transforming Business) award in 2025, and Food4Education (which she founded) was selected for the *TIME*100 Most Influential Companies in 2024.

Achieving all of this as a young Black woman entrepreneur in Africa was groundbreaking, and Wawira was only getting started. Despite all the early accolades, unlike many entrepreneurs—including myself in my early days—she didn't believe all her own press. She knew what she knew and knew what she needed to know. Her vision at the time was to create a "Robin Hood" business model where she would start a commercial catering company that would earn market rates and the profits would fund the food that she was providing kids in school who were desperate for nourishment but had no access to it. "Jim," she said, "this model will be self-sustaining and I won't need to continue to raise outside funds forever."

It was an appealing idea, and for many prospective funders it would resonate. But not for me. I knew a thing or two about catering and food service, having grown up in our family's supermarket business and later on in my thirties starting an upscale food company. What I learned was that details mattered a lot. Particularly when you are catering a special celebration, you need to be on all the time and there is little margin for error.

I worried that Wawira had oversimplified in her mind the challenges of running two businesses at the same time—one catering to upscale businesses who were inflexible, the other trying to solve for hunger in school and developing a supply chain that could serve it—and that this would not end well. I worried that the catering business failure would also reduce Wawira's gravitas and potentially stop funders from funding the critical work of getting lunches to kids in school, fundamentally reducing the amazing potential of what Wawira had already created.

Wawira heard me out and sat silent for what seemed like forever at the time and then said that she would take it to heart and get back to us. We went forward with our investment and three months later I got a call from her telling me she was closing the catering business and would focus exclusively on the school lunch efforts and that she was certain she would find the funding to make it work at scale.

Her aspiration at the time was to feed a few thousand children. Today she is feeding half a million kids every day. What made Wawira so different from others is her ability to iterate in real time and to be willing to take risks and monitor them constantly. Even more importantly, she understood as a young leader that the risks she was undertaking were not just a risk to her, but would be borne by the kids she so desperately wanted to help.

Food4Education

Children participating in the Food4Education program in Kenya.

She was focused on the children and her hope for a better future for them. How did she develop this sense of self so early? It had everything to do with her experience growing up as the child of health workers in Kenya.

You see, she saw firsthand, every day, what giving and service to others looked like when people would come to her home, or to their clinic, and her parents' faces would change when met with people in need.

They were problem-solving for their community every single day, and what Wawira saw was that their acts of service fulfilled her parents as much as they helped those in need. That service to others—what we think of as hope *realized*—is transformative to those you are serving and to yourself.

Wawira's parents never had to choose between their service to others and their ability to provide for their children. Both of these responsibilities could work together, sometimes uncomfortably, but always in support of each other. One clear example of this was in September 1995 when Wawira's father brought home a television—one of the first families in the village to have a TV. It quickly became a cherished possession in the house and was a coveted source of news and entertainment for the family. But one day when Wawira got home from school, it was gone. She was stunned.

She asked her parents what had happened and her dad was quick to explain. He told her, "Wawira, one of our neighbors needed money to buy her prescriptions, so we had to sell the TV to pay for the medication."

At first, Wawira was angry but, of course, later she came to understand. Her parents traded a small luxury for helping people. It was what they always did. They made the community's problems and needs their own—it was their extended family, something Wawira internalized at an early age.

It wasn't just that her parents were selfless; they fundamentally understood that no one lives alone and that everyone has the power to help others in need. This belief system she saw in action every day was responsible for her parents' endless well of hope for themselves and others. It was a lesson she would never forget.

Wawira attended university in Australia but longed to help her community back home in Ruiru, Kenya. She asked her parents what they thought was the biggest issue kids were having in school. Her parents told her that kids were fainting from hunger—they were lacking meals so they could not concentrate in class. "They were hungry and in need." This resonated deeply with Wawira, so much so that when she returned home from university for holidays, she decided to try to make a difference by starting a small school feeding program for a core group of 25 students she knew needed help.

She recalls her efforts. "At the first school, there was a nearby market and kids would run in to beg for food instead of staying in class. Food was so much more important than education to these children. And the emotional effect on their parents was also taking a toll. The parents felt helpless and responsible for not being able to provide for their children. And as hungry homes are often unhappy homes, domestic violence was disproportionately higher in these families. It felt hopeless."

Contrary to conventional wisdom at the time, Kenya's low educational attainment wasn't a function of a bad curriculum or incompetent teachers. It was more fundamental than that: Hungry kids can't learn.

So, in some ways, the task was actually easier to fix. Kids were already required in Kenya to be at school; what the schools lacked was food to serve the children. This was a problem Wawira knew she could fix.

And she set about doing just that.

In the beginning it was heartbreaking to see. The kids she was feeding would actually take the food home to their parents, who also needed food. So, she knew she had to do more. She had to scale this.

She steadfastly developed systems and ways to provide food at scale for hundreds of thousands of children in school.

Food4Education

Wawira Njiru poses with the first 25 children to enjoy Food4Education lunch meals in 2012.

Today, Food4Education is serving nutritious, balanced meals to 600,000 children every single day—something that was unthinkable a decade ago.

Food4Education is powering a new school feeding industry in Africa using technology and smart supply chains to source local ingredients from smallholder farmers to scale sustainable, nutritious, and affordable school feeding programs across Africa.

Within a couple years, they will feed nearly one million students every day.

Food4Education

Warm smiles and undeniable joy from those who receive a hot, nutritious cup of uji and a meal at Kimorori Primary School in Murang'a County.

Their success was a function of meeting communities and government where they were—not where they wished they would be. A continued obsession with operations and execution at the tactical level also ensures the right people are doing the right things at the right time. It may sound easy, but it's one of the hardest things for organizations to do.

Food4Education

Wawira with the Food4Education staff.

And the ripple effect of feeding these kids and alleviating their hunger is game changing.

The parents that care for these children no longer feel helpless because their children are being fed. The educational attainment level has skyrocketed as kids are staying in school and are better able to learn.

The entire Food4Education enterprise itself has created 5,000 direct jobs for the community and more across the supply chain—the farmers, the drivers, and the servers. A large portion of Wawira's staff—74%—are women hired from the communities, meaning many parents of these children are actually the ones who are cooking for them. Because the women they hired already knew how to cook, training them to cook in a commercial kitchen was seamless. It was a complete circle—the schoolchildren eating would tell their moms cooking their food how much they loved them, but, "Could you serve *chapati*?" Or, "Could you add this or that?"

Wawira hadn't created a commercial enterprise but a family enterprise with so many benefits beyond what she originally intended. These families now have stable incomes and can take care of their loved ones. Faith in the government's ability has also been restored as the community sees food delivered every day to its schools, in part paid for by the government.

Most importantly, receiving a reliable meal, day after day, means that, downstream, other mental health effects can be mitigated. When children feel insecure, the damage created is profound and not easily fixed. Not being able to rely on a steady food supply has debilitating psychological effects for a child. But those effects can be undone if addressed early on.

Jackson was one of the first 25 children Wawira fed when the program began in 2012. Back then, Jackson was 12, hungry, and small for his age, one of many faces in a long line of uncertainty.

Today, Jackson is a different person. He now stands tall in the same kitchen where he once came to eat. He wears an apron, serving meals to a new set of children who remind him of the boy he once was. He talks about moving to a new town, about getting married, about building a life and a future that once seemed unimaginable.

He is a living testament to the power of what happens when a promise is kept—in this case, that every student would be fed every single day, no matter what.

Food4Education

Jackson, one of the first 25 kids Food4Education started feeding in 2012, today stands with Wawira helping to feed the future.

In a world where so much is uncertain, Jackson found something solid to stand on. And in him, Wawira found her own reminder that hope doesn't always arrive as a miracle. Sometimes it grows slowly from one meal to the next, from one child to one man, until one day it stands before you, both thanking you for what you did for him and showing you what he can do for others.

Hope truly springs eternal.

Food4Education

Wawira Njiru surrounded by the schoolchildren now receiving nutritious lunch meals every day.

Chapter 7

Letting Love Become Healing

"At its core, this work is about honoring one of the most ancient human practices, helping those we love."

—Edith Elliott, co-CEO, Noora Health

In January 2016, Edith Elliott and her co-founder arrived in our Menlo Park office and sat at our conference room table surrounded by eight others from our team—four managing directors, three associates, and me.

The meeting was typical of the early meetings we have with our portfolio leaders and was an opportunity for our team to meet the entrepreneur in person and move past a "clinical" level of due diligence. We use these meetings to get a clearer sense of the leader as a person and for the entrepreneur to get to know us. Above all else, we want to understand the leader's commitment to the mission and their ability to persist when, inevitably, life's many challenges occur. We have learned over time how critical it is to invest in leaders who, when confronted with difficult moments, stay the course, don't back down, and always, always lean in.

At first, we had some skepticism about Edith's startup. The idea came from a project in a Stanford class, Design for Extreme Affordability, where students are asked to take on a real-world problem and create a solution. Would this class project really have legs? As we would learn, Edith and her team were the real deal. And Noora Health's early days reinforced that. She and her three cofounders from the class project attracted advisors from Stanford and were invited to be a part of the 2014 Winter Cohort of Y Combinator, a well-known startup accelerator in Silicon Valley, where venture capitalists provide funding, mentorship, and resources to early-stage startups. Companies like Airbnb, Coinbase, DoorDash, and Instacart came out of Y Combinator. The invitation to join their cohort was a further confirmation that the Noora team was onto something.

As she sat with us, she explained that they were tackling the high readmissions rate and shortage of nursing staff in Indian hospitals by training family members who were waiting in the hospitals while their loved ones were in surgery to perform postoperative care.

Their vision was to redefine the standard of care and create another method—another tool in the tool kit—for low- and middle-income patients. What she didn't say, because she thought we might dismiss it even though she knew it to be true, was that their model was *powered by love.*

Simply stated, they were leveraging the urgency and determination of family members to do everything they could to help their loved ones recover and end the hopelessness that these family members often felt. You see, underneath it all, Noora Health was powered by the same love that Edith had witnessed as she watched her mother and the key people in her life act as caregivers to someone else they loved deeply. No moment was more powerful than the one in the summer of 1997 when Edith was 13, watching her mom take care of her best friend, Robert, who was dying from HIV. Watching her mom be at Robert's side day and night was something she will never forget. That same summer, Edith's mother had brain surgery, and Edith stepped in to help care for her mother with the same limitless determination and steadfast care to help her recover and heal.

She then watched her mom and her aunts take care of her grandmother. Woven throughout Edith's life was a consistent thread of caring for and being taken care of very deeply. It gave her comfort knowing that caregiving is going to come back to her if and when she needs it.

Edith Elliott

Edith and her mother.

Her experience of having watched Robert's struggle with HIV drove Edith to want to understand more of what was happening in the world around this disease, and she discovered that global health is impacted at a large scale based on the decisions of a few people. For her, this asymmetry—huge swaths of populations affected by the decisions of a few individuals—was a head-scratcher. She wondered how this had come to be.

As she dove deeply into this work, she was reminded time and time again that while the decisions of a few affected many, often a person close to someone who was sick could make all the difference in the world in terms of outcomes and how the disease progression affected the individual.

It was this realization that made the thread of her experiences throughout her life become clear.

She believed that with Noora Health she and her team could change the lives of millions of people by helping them as caregivers for their loved ones, regardless of economic capacity or medical training. At its core, the work was simply about honoring the most ancient—and most human—instinct to help those we love and leveraging that love to rethink health care.

Ten years after its founding, Noora Health has scaled to more than 16,000 hospitals and clinics in India, Bangladesh, Indonesia, and Nepal and trained more than 50 million family caregivers and patients. And there is no end to the need for its services.

Globally, there will be a shortage of nearly 11 million health care workers by 2030.[5] The systems are overburdened with life and death consequences for patients.

Noora Health

Lead trainer Parveen turns a hospital hallway into a classroom in Jamalpur, Karnataka, India.

Every year in South Asia alone, nearly 1.3 million children under five die.[6] And far too many of these

---

5 "Health Workforce," World Health Organization, www.who.int/health-topics/health-workforce#tab=tab_1.

6 "Fewer Children Dying Before Turning Five in Southern Asian Than Ever Before—UNICEF," UNICEF, March 13, 2024, www.unicef.org/rosa/press-releases/fewer-children-dying-turning-five-southern-asia-ever.

deaths can be prevented with better health practices at home.

Noora Health trains and equips families and works with hospitals and clinics to meet people where they are—at the patient's bedside, in the hallways, in the waiting areas.

Noora Health trains nurses so that they can run sessions with groups of families to teach them actionable skills—things like wound care and how to recognize warning signs like jaundice in a newborn or slurred speech in a cardiac patient. And they leave plenty of time for questions and demonstrations. Once patients and families leave the hospital, Noora Health stays connected with them, sending them messages, videos, and reminders that are relevant for their loved ones. Whether it's new parents or surgical or oncology patients, they've seen that this approach works across all types of care. Because the common thread is that "loved ones are there, and they want to help."

Noora Health has reached tens of thousands of hospitals and clinics, helping them change the way they deliver care. And the results are clear. They have seen that "this program reduces cardiac surgery complications by 71%, and our early data suggests that it reduces newborn deaths by 18%. That would mean that over nine babies' lives are saved for every 1,000 live births. And it's all happening at an extremely low cost because the solution leverages existing resources."[7]

In their TED Talk, Edith and her cofounder Shahed Alam, MD, talk about one patient who was impacted—a young man named Bino, who had heart surgery at the nearest major hospital to him, in Kolkata. "He was accompanied by his wife Sunita and his uncle, and both of them went through the training. Later on, when I visited them in their home, Sunita had just wrapped up Bino's wound care, commenting how she left it undressed, just like in the training. She showed me how she used the thermometers and how she checked Bino's pulse and rattled off all the normal ranges for blood pressure, heart rate, and temperature. She told me that they eat more fish now instead of red meat, and avoided foods with too much vitamin K because of his new medication. His uncle told me that they were able to avoid going to the local clinic every single time they needed to do

---

7 Edith Elliott and Shahed Alam, "The Most Powerful Untapped Resource in Health Care," May 2, 2022, https://www.ted.com/talks/edith_elliott_and_shahed_alam_the_most_powerful_untapped_resource_in_health_care/tr.

basic wound care. This saved them travel and also a dollar-fifty per visit. This is a huge amount for a family that had to sell a part of their property to finance the operation. Now Sunita never got the opportunity to learn how to read or write, but hundreds of kilometers from the nearest major hospital, she confidently led Bino's recovery."[8]

Gabriel Diamond, The Skoll Foundation

Edith Elliott and Shahed Alam, co-founders and co-CEOs of Noora Health, in 2021.

In every caregiver Noora Health trains, Edith sees the determination and triumph of her own family caring for each other, powered by their love.

8 Elliott and Alam, "The Most Powerful Untapped Resource in Health Care."

Noora Health

Nurses enjoy a moment together following a Care Companion Program session at Shishu Hospital in Dhaka, Bangladesh.

In the early days of Noora Health, Edith discovered something surprising. In her professional life, she felt dogged by a continual competition for donors, resources, and recognition.

Even in an organization whose key tool is care, the reality of scarce resources and time was taking its toll on her and her family.

And then something unexpected happened to her.

One of her significant donors asked her a question she wasn't expecting to come from him. "Edith," he said, "how are you doing? Are you happy? Do you want to have children?" Those questions set off an emotional response. The donor wasn't just interested in how Noora Health was doing; he wanted to make sure that she was okay. It was a timely question as Edith and her husband had been struggling to build a family.

The donor wasn't asking her how she was doing to just make sure she could do more work. The donor made sure Edith and her family were prioritizing their family and, most important, had what they needed to make that happen. Because an organization in service to others needs to be sure it's taking care of itself. Finding this form of care in her work life showed Edith something that fundamentally changed how she led Noora Health.

This gave Edith the opportunity and freedom to prioritize care for herself and her team in ways she had not imagined. To see that she could lead her professional life with compassion and vulnerability opened the door for her to fully describe the power of Noora Health's model—it was truly a circle powered by love.

Edith described in her TED Talk, "It's that dogged determination to get your aging mom's meds sorted out, that tenacious energy to get your kid to the ER. Like oxygen, it is essential to our health and our well-being. It is ever-present, but invisible. It's the fuel of family advocacy. And for too long it's either been seen as a nuisance or it's been ignored altogether within health care settings. Noora Health was founded on the shared belief that love is the most powerful, untapped resource available. And when valued and made visible, it can transform health systems."

Edith and the Noora team show that love, demonstrated by authentic care, is the engine of hope. It makes us believe in better days, even when we can't yet see them.

Chapter 8

If Not Me, Who?

"This is what we do—we help."

—Jared Walker, CEO, Dollar For

By now you might be thinking, *I can never do what these people have done*. But that's not true. Each of us has the ability to make a difference in the world, and one of our entrepreneurs shows just that. It's Jared Walker, the founder and CEO of Dollar For. Homeschooled from an early age, Jared would later drop out of college with only one class left to take. He worked as a bartender and server. But Jared had the best education in the world from the best person who could teach him: his mom, Christine.

Understated in every way, Christine knew what life was all about and taught her children through her actions. Like so many of the great teachers in the world, learning is about doing, and that is exactly what she encouraged her children to do.

Jared was one of five siblings and to this day has never forgotten the lessons he learned as a six-year-old. Piled into his mom's car with his siblings every week, she drove them to weekly visits to see her sister. They didn't grow up with much, and family mattered, so what they did have Christine found a way to share with those in need.

But these weren't just trips to get from point A to point B. They were intentional lessons she wanted her family to learn. She wanted them to notice the life that was around them with all its positives and all its inequities. On these weekly visits, Christine would often pull over to check on the same homeless man and talk.

Jared didn't know his name or his story. He only knew that his mother saw him and cared for him. In fact, before each trip, she would pack a lunch for the man on the corner and give it to him. It wasn't an announcement; it was a ritual.

To a six-year-old, the act didn't yet have the language of compassion or social justice. It was just what his mother did—seeing someone's pain and doing something, however small, to ease it. But for Jared, that gesture became the first spark of what he would later describe as hope for humanity. And he learned the lesson, the visit, wasn't about the lunch. It was about the noticing. She didn't drive past; she stopped.

Her small, consistent kindness planted a seed within Jared—a conviction that the world could be better if people simply cared enough to *act*.

Dollar For

A young Jared Walker with his mom, Christine.

In April 2012, Jared was 23 and sitting at home in Portland, Oregon, with his wife when she got a phone call. Her aunt had passed away from cancer. Just 20 minutes later, Jared got a phone call that his cousin had gone into labor seven weeks premature, and the baby needed heart surgery to live. That's two of his relatives' families being hit with medical emergencies in less than an hour. In that moment the number one question everyone in his family had was not, "Are you okay?" or "Do you have what you need to take care of yourself and your family?" Instead, it was, "How the heck are we gonna pay for it?"

Jared began to understand their experience wasn't an anomaly—one in four Americans avoid the care they need because of the cost. For the approximately 188 million Americans barely making ends meet, a medical emergency can push them into a downward spiral of poverty. One in five American households have medical debt, totaling an estimated $220 billion. And medical bills are the number one cause of bankruptcy in the United States.

So, Jared started helping the only way he knew how. First by organizing local grassroots events at coffee shops where the money raised would help to pay for someone's unpaid medical bills in his community. At one of the events, Jared met a man named Eli, who told him about section 501(r) of the Affordable Care Act, which stated that in order to keep their tax exempt status, hospitals have to have charity care policies that reduce or even completely forgive your hospital bills if you meet certain income requirements. Jared thought it sounded too good to be true, but Eli was right. The problem was no one knew this existed. Few hospitals ever tell patients about these policies or how to access them. Yet people were going into bankruptcy over medical bills and the hospitals let them.

Dollar For

Dollar For helps families across the country reduce or eliminate medical debt.

Jared investigated how patients could access these policies and he quickly began volunteering to fill out applications for people. Within a few months, $1 million of medical debt disappeared for people in Portland.

Jared wanted to scream it from the rooftops.

He pitched journalists, news agencies, and radio shows, but no one would listen and no one picked up his story. Later that month at the Thanksgiving table, Jared's little sister told him to post it on TikTok. Jared was skeptical but he downloaded the app anyway, recorded a video explaining charity care policies, and posted it. He didn't have any followers, and yet what happened next changed Jared's life. The post went viral—garnering 30 million views—and from there, Dollar For was born.

Jared created the only database in existence with information on every hospital in the country and their charity care eligibility criteria and application process.

Years later, it's this same conviction that became the foundation for Dollar For. But Dollar For didn't come from a perfect business plan. It grew from persistence.

Jared's story isn't one of straight lines or shiny credentials—he'll be the first to tell you that. While he did initially drop out of college one course short, he took that final class and received his degree in 2024 as an already established CEO. That's the thing about him—he's authentic to the core, real, and, like his mom, willing to stop and fix the problems he sees right outside his own door.

Since that first viral video, Dollar For has become

a national force, submitting more than 40,000 financial assistance applications and eliminating more than $130 million in medical debt for people across the country—a number that is climbing every day.

Every minute, Jared's work changes the trajectory of someone's life.

Take Gabriela, for instance, who was faced with the decision to pay a hospital bill or continue her education. Gabriela found Dollar For and, as a result, graduated from college with a clean bill of health.

Or Sammy, who had to decide between paying his rent or a hospital bill. Today, Sammy has a stable living situation because of Dollar For and is able to envision a different future.

Or Carlos, who moved to Boston to get his master's degree and was soon diagnosed with Hodgkin lymphoma. He didn't have insurance and had to leave his job to receive treatment. With hospital bills piling up, Carlos didn't know how he was going to pay for his rent, his food, or even his life. Carlos reached out to Jared and his $3,000 balance was eliminated. Carlos was able to focus on his treatment and today is cancer free.

By 2028, Dollar For will, as Jared says, "crush" $1 billion of debt for 175,000 individual patients and drive comprehensive policy reform in targeted states. Securing policy wins in California, Texas, and Oregon to ensure hospitals are responsible for providing financial assistance to qualified patients could eliminate up to $3.3 billion of medical debt every year.

During a recent speech at our annual DRK retreat, Jared stood before a room full of his peers and shared this very story. But as he concluded, he stunned the audience by adding, "Since I began speaking nine minutes ago, here are a few real-time updates of people whose debt has been relieved in this short time." Then he grabbed his phone and began reading them aloud one by one: "$2,000 . . . $3,700 . . . $2,000 . . . $3,600 . . . $1,700 . . . $9,100 . . . $168,000 . . . $32,000 . . . $136." The room was silent in awe.

Vince Tarry, iClickStudios

Jared Walker speaks to an audience of 200+ social impact entrepreneurs during the DRK Foundation Annual Retreat in Menlo Park, California, in 2025.

In fact, on a recent call I had with Jared, he paused mid-story to read a notification from his phone: another $231,000 medical bill waived in Flagstaff, Arizona. "That's a big one," he murmured, almost to himself.

And those are just a few examples of the immense impact Jared is making in the lives of those who need it the most.

But even as Dollar For scales, he still traces its roots to those drives with his mother. Her quiet insistence that kindness isn't a theory; it's a practice. "She was just so intentional," he says. "It wasn't performative. It was just what you do. You notice suffering, and you do something about it."

That early lesson stayed with him through every setback, every doubt, every small donation that barely seemed to make a dent. "Even at a young age," he says, "you can see how the world beats people up. And seeing my mom take action against that gave me hope. Like, okay, this is what we do. We help."

It's easy to see the through line now: from a sandwich shared with one man to a nonprofit that changes the lives of millions. From one woman's compassion to her son's mission. What began as a small act of kindness became a legacy—a belief that even the smallest things, when done with care, can ripple out into something far greater.

I see the same thing in all our entrepreneurs—they are called to service and every one of them was drawn to it by someone in their life. They don't see themselves as visionaries or leaders. None of that is relevant to them; frankly, they couldn't care less.

But when I sit down with each of them for the first time, I see the same selfless commitment to helping someone else. And though each of their paths to get where they are is different, they all have gotten there with a rare blend of humility, conviction, resilience, and purpose that tells me, without question: This person is going to make a difference.

Chapter 9

Moving Hope to Action—The Playbook

"It's not that I'm so smart; it's just that I stay with problems longer."

—Albert Einstein

The stories in the previous chapters demonstrate how one person literally changed the course of millions of lives by transforming hope into action. But how exactly did they do it?

That's the number one question I get asked when I speak on panels and at conferences. Believe me, I used to ask the same question myself. And without a playbook, every problem seemed overwhelming. But like most challenges in life, every problem can be unpacked.

The entrepreneurs introduced in the previous chapters were able to translate their belief systems into action by deeply investigating the nature of the problem or constraint that was causing the harm. They had a "start" agenda that gave them a blueprint to create the imagined world they envisioned would solve the problem. They examined the existing infrastructure that surrounded the problem, enabling them to leverage parts of existing systems that could be re-enabled to deliver the change they wanted.

In this chapter, we describe the playbook—the specific tactics that these and other DRK leaders have used over and over again to translate their hope into sustainable action.

It's a blueprint that translates across all sectors and all geographies that anyone can follow.

I think of this as a framework that has five specific actionable steps.

1. Understand—and by that I mean *deeply understand*—the nature of the problem you are trying to solve; don't stop on the surface. Don't stop with the symptoms of the problem;

look for the root causes that created it. They are often hiding in plain sight.

2. Analyze the ecosystem surrounding the problem, including all the dependencies and codependencies that will need to be reordered to change the status quo, and look carefully for what exists—what we refer to as the "plumbing" or the existing infrastructure—that can be repurposed. In this effort, don't let perfection be the enemy of good. Even if an existing system isn't fully functional or delivering exactly the right services, it still exists and can be repurposed to deliver what you want it to deliver. Rarely do new systems or new technologies need to be created.
3. Develop an understanding of the resources required to solve the problem—financial and human—and the likely source of those resources on a sustained basis and define what your endgame is. In other words, what does success look like?
4. Then, critically develop your execution strategy—what do you do first, second, third, and so on; what are your short-term and long-term tactics; and who are the right people on your team who need to be in the right places,

doing the right things at the right time? Success in translating hope to action is all about execution. Ideas are great, but they never come to life without great execution.

5. And finally, know who needs to ultimately adopt your solution to embed or institutionalize it, and have a plan—and partners—to empower them to do that. After more than 270 investments in social enterprises trying to solve complex societal problems, we have seen people make a big difference in even the most intractable problems by deploying a rigorous discipline that unpacks these five things regardless of sector or geography.

1. Understand the nature of the problem you are trying to solve.

The first step is always identifying the problem in detail. That sounds obvious, but many organizations start too broad—such as, we're going to "solve poverty" or "end climate change"—and then they can't make progress because they never defined which part of the problem they were actually tackling. Success starts with deeply understanding the issue, its constraints, and the web of interdependencies around it.

To unpack a problem, I like to use Paul Brest's "big cube" versus "small cube" framework.[9] Imagine a giant Rubik's Cube. A big cube problem is something like climate change—massive, interconnected, and requiring coordination across borders, sectors, and generations. No one person or single organization can fix it. On the other hand, a small cube problem is fully within your control. Cleaning up a neighborhood block, for instance, can be done by one individual and it can be measured, completed, and left behind knowing it was done, but its impact is limited and will rarely last.

Most real-world challenges fall somewhere in between. And here's the rub: Funders, understandably, are drawn to the small cubes. They're neat and solvable, and you can show results quickly. But the big, systemic challenges tend to languish because they're harder, messier, and longer-term investments. So, the first question to ask yourself is: What size cube am I working on, and what does that mean for the resources I'll need?

In Food4Education's case, Wawira was solving for how to help kids do well in school. She wasn't solving for the whole educational system in Kenya—kids

---

9 Paul Brest and Hal Harvey, *Money Well Spent: A Strategic Plan for Smart Philanthropy* (Bloomberg Press, 2008).

were already required to come to school; they just weren't being fed. The solution leveraged the system, which already required them to come to school. She just needed to develop, at scale, a way to feed them because, as you saw, hungry kids can't learn. So by feeding them in school, she got them to stay in school *and* learn.

2. Analyze the ecosystem that surrounds it and the existing infrastructure that can be reused.

Rarely are completely new systems needed. Even rarer do they succeed. They are incredibly capital intensive and costly, they take forever to build, and as a result they are inherently risky, often ultimately dooming a social enterprise from the beginning by sapping its precious resources.

By investing serious time mapping and understanding the existing ecosystem (institutions, dependencies, channels) before proposing new systems, you can better understand what exists and what is missing. Look specifically at what elements of the existing infrastructure aren't working and try to identify how they can be repurposed to better serve the intended population.

Intentionally working within and trying to repurpose existing systems, infrastructure, and resources can achieve deeper, more sustainable impact at lower cost. Leverage can come in many forms: linking, strengthening, filling gaps, or making existing institutions more effective. Such strategies tend to be lower risk, more cost-effective, and more resilient to political shifts, since they don't rely on new legislation. And they dramatically de-risk execution by finding leverage points within existing systems.

Figure 1 shows one such landscaping analysis, focusing on access to criminal justice and visually depicting the problem in context.

Once completed, you can see what specific actions are needed to unlock the binding constraint and open new access points—meeting people where they are; fixing so-called trap doors between institutions where handoffs are supposed to take place but often fall through the cracks; embedding new service offerings to existing distribution systems in existing institutions; and catalyzing data to help decision-makers execute their responsibilities faster, with more cost effectiveness, and with better outcomes for their constituencies.

Recidiviz is a good example of deploying data to help decision-makers. By collecting critical data that these agencies needed to do their jobs, Clem and the team were able to help the agency heads and their case managers and parole officers surface eligible individuals for release, reduce caseloads, and drive better outcomes for their constituencies. Recidiviz isn't trying to change the criminal justice system; it's helping improve the existing systems by giving users the data they need—and want—to do their jobs. No new laws needed; no new authorities required.

Another example is a health care nonprofit that realized that many people eligible for health care access were either "invisible" to the providers in the system or the providers' system was inaccessible to them.

Rather than creating a new infrastructure to locate these folks, they looked instead at where people were already gathering—laundromats, barbershops, food banks, community centers, churches—to connect individuals to existing programs.

They piggybacked on existing infrastructure, filling gaps without reinventing the wheel. The key was not creating a new health system, but enabling connections between people and existing service providers.

Another nonprofit is doing the same thing but for a different population, namely college students in community colleges and state universities. Most of these students are eligible for benefits that can make

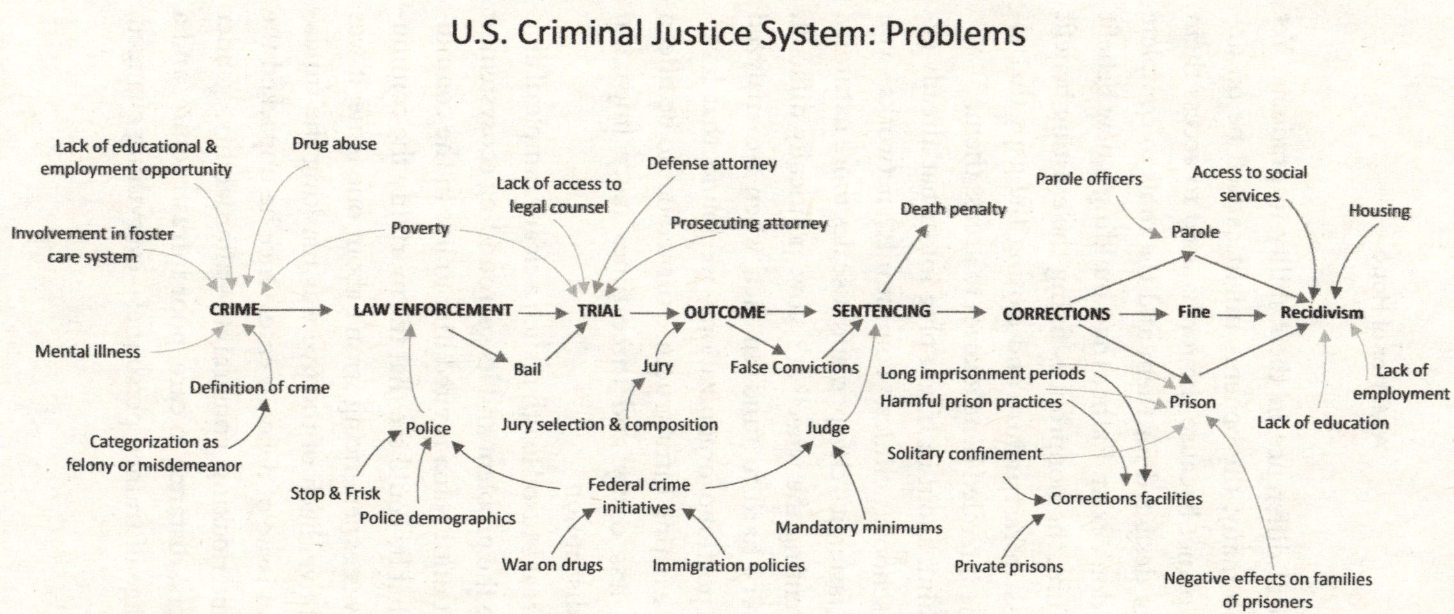

DRK Foundation

Figure 1. US Criminal Justice Mapping

a critical difference in their ability to graduate. Yet for too many, the benefits might as well be on another planet because the forms used to access them are not designed for them and the tools to complete them don't exist. Rather than building a new benefit structure, the nonprofit is fixing the existing benefit process infrastructure and closing the gaps that allow the intended beneficiaries to access them.

Think about it: If you plug into what already exists—schools, clinics, community networks—you move faster, it's cheaper, and it scales more naturally. Reinventing the wheel? It's slow, politically difficult, and very hard to fund. In fact, when we analyzed DRK portfolio organizations, we found that leveraging existing infrastructure turned out to be fifteen times less costly and three times more impactful than disruption.

Ari at Muso Health is such a clear example of analyzing the problem and its surrounding ecosystem. It wasn't until Nana invited him to live in the community that he could see that the mortality the community was experiencing wasn't about one issue; it was about five. Each of the five was masking the fundamental issue of delay in care. Once he unpacked the five interlocking constraints—affordability, gender barriers, distance to care, poor infrastructure, and a shortage of trained personnel—everything changed.

But they all had to be done *and in the right sequence.* If you fixed one but ignored the others, the system was still broken. But by sequencing carefully—first lowering the cost of drugs, then addressing gender access, then transportation, then facilities, then staff—he saw treatment rates soar and costs plummet. That's sequencing in action.

3. Develop an understanding of the resources required to solve the problem, the source of those resources, and the endgame.

It's essential to understand in the beginning what your "endgame" is.[10] What happens if you succeed? How will you know early on what your progress is toward that endgame and how can you measure it along the way? Equally important to understand is what resources are required to reach the endgame and who is going to fund your efforts. Without this map to a destination, organizations often start running without knowing where the finish line is. They have energy, passion, maybe even funding, but no

10 Gugelev, Alice and Stern, Andrew, "What's your Endgame?" *Stanford Social Innovation Review,* Winter 2015. https://ssir.org/articles/entry/whats_your_endgame.

clarity about what they're ultimately aiming for. And without that clarity, it's hard to build a strategy. Different endgames require different levels of resources.

Now, here's the thing—we're not saying you need to know the "right" endgame from the start. Chances are, you'll be wrong. But even a working hypothesis is invaluable because it forces you to orient your activities toward something concrete.

For EducationSuperHighway, Evan started with a finite goal—to close the "classroom connectivity gap" in US public schools, where in 2013 only about 30% of students had adequate internet for digital learning. Rather than building a new infrastructure from scratch, he focused on mapping the problem and leveraging existing systems. He launched the National School Speed Test, collecting data from tens of thousands of schools to reveal huge disparities in bandwidth and pricing. This data-driven approach highlighted inefficiencies in the market and became the foundation for advocacy and partnerships aimed at making high-speed internet affordable and accessible for all schools. Working closely with state governments, school districts, and internet service providers, EducationSuperHighway helped modernize the FCC's E-Rate program, which subsidizes internet access for schools. The modernization prioritized broadband and Wi-Fi upgrades, increased funding, and introduced state matching programs for fiber construction. They also developed practical tools like "Compare & Connect K–12," enabling districts to benchmark pricing and negotiate better deals, while providing hands-on consulting support to help schools design, fund, and execute infrastructure upgrades.

By 2019, EducationSuperHighway had effectively achieved its mission: 99% of US public schools gained access to high-speed broadband, and the cost of internet access dropped by about 90% compared to 2013. Their success underscored the power of leveraging existing systems, data transparency, and cross-sector collaboration over disruptive innovation. Instead of replacing government programs or creating parallel systems, they worked within the existing policy and infrastructure landscape to make it more efficient, equitable, and scalable—a model of systemic change built on partnership and optimization rather than disruption.

With unprecedented, bipartisan effort by federal, state, and school district leaders, supported by EducationSuperHighway and advocacy organizations, the classroom connectivity gap is now closed. Forty-seven million students are connected, and 99.7% of US schools have a high-speed broadband connection.

Having completed their mission, EducationSuper-Highway 1.0 sunsetted in August 2020.

4. Critically develop your execution strategy—what do you do first, second, and third and how do you make sure you have the right people in the right places doing the right things at the right time?

It's easy to have good ideas. Turning good ideas into real, sustained action is much more difficult. To do so, you need to balance near-term and long-term tactics. Short-term targets are actionable in the near term, can be achieved in short time frames, are easily measured, require limited codependencies, and, because success is likely, provide initial gravitas and momentum, making them brand enhancing.

Long-term targets require a longer time frame, capture the largest aspirations, and often deal with the "meta" problem. Successfully solving for these types of problems relates directly to first solving the smaller targets. Over time, multiple shorter-term tactics—in the aggregate—lead to solving the larger problem.

Organizations often fall into the trap of only talking about the big, systemic changes they want, without offering credible short-term interventions.

But credibility is fragile, and short-term wins build it.

You need to be able to show measurable progress quickly, even if it's just on one piece of the puzzle. That credibility gives you the runway to pursue longer-term ambitions. Solve the pieces you control first, show quick wins, and save the bigger systemic fights for later, when your credibility is stronger. Don't waste energy charging into battles where every force is aligned against you.

And don't forget about organizational capacity. Over and over again, we see social enterprises constrained by their failure to have the right people doing the right things at the right time. And recognizing every choice you make, or don't make, has consequences. Many entrepreneurs put off hiring key people. They say, "We'll wait until we're bigger," or "We can't afford it yet." But the cost of waiting is huge—missed opportunities, lost momentum. The truth is, you need to hire around yourself. Find people who like to do the critical tasks you don't like to do or are not good at. Not a numbers person? Then find one. Not a great people person? Hire one. You see the point: The sooner you bring in the right people, the more resilient and capable your organization will be and, as a result, the faster you'll grow and the more impact you'll have.

Even more importantly, enterprises that have the right people in place are far more resilient to crises.

As one of my mentors, Sue Gordon, who was the deputy director of national intelligence and held multiple leadership roles at the CIA and knows a thing or two about crises, told me, leadership is all about knowing what you know and what you don't know. Too often, she explained, leaders think they know everything and disregard other views. Resilient organizations are packed with people who see the world differently from each other but believe deeply in the organization's mission. And when confronted with crises, these organizations don't shake their "fists" at the cosmos, as Sue refers to it; instead, they move into two simultaneous modes—analysis about what caused the crisis to start with and action to mitigate it. And all the research on leadership backs this up. Teams with different skills and views outperform teams that think alike.

And finally, proximity—physical or experiential—matters when navigating complex problems. Organizations that stay close to the communities they serve or are packed with people either from the community or those who have experienced the problem the organization is working to fix tend to make better decisions, faster, because they know the nuances of the problem and its codependencies. As a result, their boards, staff, and leaders are grounded in lived experience, not just abstract or remote "fly-in" strategy.

5. Know who needs to ultimately adopt your solution to embed or institutionalize it, and have a plan–and partners–to do that.

Finally, it's always, always about who is going to adopt your solution. Impact is not about building clever tools; it's about making sure those tools actually get used.

As Clem showed, a parole officer with 200 cases isn't going to implement a brilliant new framework unless it helps them prioritize what matters most.

Reaching a scale of users is all about understanding human behavior and processes and designing for the messy reality of human use, not some idealized version.

As shown in earlier chapters, adoption at ultimate scale starts with making sure what you are building is useful to those who need it. And, equally important, that someone is willing to pay for it. One deeply engaged customer is worth far more than five casual ones. Underpricing is a trap: It signals low value, prevents you from raising prices later, and undermines sustainability. Testing true willingness to pay—whether in dollars, effort, or adoption—proves demand more effectively than handing something out cheaply.

Noora Health, responding to a huge shortage of nursing staff in India, implemented a family training program that reduced readmission rates, improved patient and caregiver experience and retention, dramatically improved community-level outcomes, and increased nurses' efficiency.

The program was not just good for families and didn't just provide better care for patients; it helped hospitals become more efficient by supplementing nursing shortages with trained family members.

Even in the public-run hospitals (government-run facilities providing free care for the very poor) in India, they expected the adoption process to be arduous and lengthy but instead found it to be quick and even easier to roll out than in private hospitals, because the public-run hospitals needed the increased efficiency even more than the private hospitals. This quick adoption led to a partnership with the World Health Organization to scale their family caregiver training model globally as a standard component of health care delivery.

Adoption almost always involves building social capital and movement. The status quo is incredibly resistant to change. In creating tailwinds it's important to recognize that there is a real difference between "stop energy" and "start energy." It's relatively easy to rally people around stopping something—a bad law, a harmful practice, an unpopular company. It's much harder to mobilize consensus around building something new.

Adoption rarely takes place as a result of telling folks how bad something that exists is.

As Jared at Dollar For demonstrated, you need to provide real proof of the counterfactual—the imagined new reality you are offering—showing how it can be readily accessed, and that it works. By creating this awareness, two things happen at once: Folks who need the help get it and the institutions that were formerly the obstacle become part of the solution. Provided this proof, there is simply too much social awareness of the issue and its solution by the public to ignore.

And don't make perfection the enemy of good. Rarely is a solution without flaws but, as you have seen throughout the book, solutions need not be perfect to work.

The most important thing is to be doing something to fix a problem now. If your solution works and is helping hundreds and then thousands of people, it's good enough. Too often, entrepreneurs never act because they want their solution to be perfect in every detail. That never happens, because as solutions scale, new, unforeseeable issues arise. That's OK because solving complex issues requires continual learning and modifications.

Equally important to not letting perfection be the enemy of good is not demonizing folks who don't agree with you or who oppose your solution.

This was another key lesson Evan learned in the beginning of EducationSuperHighway. Early on, there was plenty of opposition to what ESH was trying to do. After all, lots of folks are often vested in the status quo.

Change is difficult. The ESH team was constantly frustrated by folks who ignored what the data was telling them. But they found a work-around—they gave everyone, including the folks who initially opposed them, frequent and public credit for the work as it became obvious that the data was right and that they were able to connect students to broadband.

It was a lesson that became a core part of how ESH went about its work. They got nearly every governor in the United States to sign on to their plan regardless of how much or how little they had done before to solve this issue. And then they gave the governors credit for seeing the problem and working to improve broadband in schools. They gave the FCC the data they needed to take credit for the impact of modernizing the E-Rate program on school connectivity. They even got the major wireless carriers a mention in one of Obama's State of the Union addresses as part of convincing them to donate hundreds of millions of dollars of free wireless broadband for kids to use at home. It was a strategy that worked over and over again, and kept key stakeholders wanting to do more to help.

Finally, persistence and alignment with tailwinds often determine whether change endures. Ground-up solutions that embed themselves within existing systems are harder to undo, even amid political upheaval. Sometimes disruption is necessary—but the most scalable wins usually come from working with constraints and finding leverage.

In the end, translating hope to action requires the five actions described previously: a deep grasp of the problem, understanding the ecosystem that surrounds it, clarity on the endgame and resources required, a tactical strategy that maximizes near-term wins, and, finally, adoption. That's how hope for a better world brings that better world to reality.

No magic wand or legion of superheroes needed. Just discipline, intentionality, great execution, and perseverance.

Chapter 10

Hope Is Everywhere

"What ultimately allows courageous people to take action isn't their lack of fear but their ability to make sense of situations in helpful ways, and also see themselves as strong, capable people who can control their destinies."

—Ranjay Gulati, *How to Be Bold*[11]

Hope is in every one of us. Some of you who have read the chapters about Ari, Clem, Kiah, Aimée, Evan, Wawira, Edith, and Jared might conclude that

11 Ranjay Gulati, "Finding the Courage to Be Bold in the Face of Fear," Harvard Business School, September 20, 2025, https://www.library.hbs.edu/working-knowledge/finding-the-courage-to-be-bold-in-the-face-of-fear.

you could never do the things that these folks have done—that creating change in the world we are living in requires superheroes to make it happen. But that's not true.

Most of the change that has taken place in the world has been achieved by folks just like you and me. Not superheroes, but folks with an enduring sense of hope and empathy for others.

And hope is often found in unexpected ways, often in the same room as sadness and despair. I want to tell you about an experience that left an enduring impact on me.

I had just flown into Boston from Virginia. As I entered the terminal, I saw a young man in surgical garb standing next to three large square white boxes. Literally hundreds of people were walking past him—ear pods in, eyes looking at their phones, rushing to get somewhere, and taking no notice of him or the boxes or why he was there by the gate. And yet, he was the anomaly in this otherwise predictable scene. But something made me take notice and I walked closer to him.

As I approached him, I noticed that on the side of the largest white plastic box, the words "MGH Cardiac Surgery Unit" were written, and the box had a number of active monitoring devices. I then realized that a live heart was in the box and that the box was being flown from Massachusetts General Hospital to someone waiting for a transplant.

At that moment I felt the intense sadness and loss that the family of the organ donor must have been feeling now, having just lost someone they loved; but at the same time, I felt the enormous joy and hope that the family of the heart recipient must have been feeling now as they anxiously awaited a new heart to arrive to save the life of their loved one.

The juxtaposition of those two powerful feelings stopped me cold as I realized that every experience each of us encounters always has two versions—one that can kindle our fears or sadness but also one of equal force that can drive our sense of hope and purpose.

In some ways, this encounter at the airport captures the essence of this book. Life is truly what each of us makes of it. And while no one gets a free pass from moments of sadness and life events that challenge our beliefs, these moments do not have to end in despair. They can also be opportunities for hope. And if you look around, you'll see that there are so many examples of this.

Take the experience of Dr. Charles Daniels, Jr., founder of Fathers' UpLift. Charles's early years were full of sadness and despair. As a child, he was rebellious and got in trouble a lot. And yet, at a single moment, his life changed. One hot and muggy day, 10-year-old Charles found himself in a chapel. He was called to the front of the church by his pastor, Edward Lumpkin. The suit he was wearing stuck to his body as he slowly approached the front of the church. He saw all the other children who were being baptized that day, together with their smiling families in the audience. But for Charles, there was no smiling family in the room. His dad had left him long ago.

When it was his turn, the pastor gestured for Charles to come over to him. He put his arms around Charles's shoulder, and they each turned to face the congregation. He asked one question that would forever change Charles and the destinies of many young children to come. "Where is the family that will stand for this boy?"

The congregation was packed to capacity. Yet no one stood but Charles's mother. She stood awkwardly by herself, reinforcing the loneliness that had defined Charles's life growing up. And then the pastor called out again, louder and more forcefully, "I said, where's the family that will stand for this boy?"

And then, without any prompting, the entire congregation stood.

And from that day on, they held Charles in their arms and did not let him go—not that day, or for years to come.

They made a vow that they would stand in the gap where Charles's father should have been. They didn't have to stand that day, but they did. And their collective action changed the life of this 10-year-old boy who would go on to build an organization that would stand up for all the other fatherless boys and girls in the world and help them and their fathers show up again. A simple act of kindness on a hot and muggy Sunday not only changed one boy's life, but in turn that young boy changed the lives of thousands of young boys and girls.

Dr. Charles Daniels, Jr.

Dr. Charles Daniels, Jr. with wife Samantha Fils-Daniels, son Clayton Daniels, and daughter SaMya Grace Daniels.

Another example is Ruth Simmons, who I've had the honor of getting to know well over the past 10 years. In every way, Ruth is extraordinary.

Ruth was the youngest of 12 children born to sharecropping parents in Grapeland, Texas. As Ruth described her early understanding of life in her recent memoir,

> Although I did not by any means witness firsthand the worst of what my parents and the rest of my family experienced in Grapeland, I was certainly made aware that being Black enclosed me in a web of stereotypes, which I would not likely escape. I had no thought that I would be exempt from the treatment my parents recounted from their past. To avoid being overtaken by the circumstances I had inherited, I had to imagine a different world . . . much as one might stubbornly build a castle in the sand, knowing that it will be washed away. But I never expected my imagined castles to permanently replace the reality of rural East Texas in the '40s and '50s.[12]

With a lot of help from family members and caring teachers, Ruth had her first glimpse of hope when

---

12 Ruth J. Simmons, *Up Home: One Girl's Journey* (Random House, 2023), 21.

she had the opportunity to attend Wellesley College in Massachusetts.

> I had arrived in Massachusetts without proper clothing for the climate . . . A local host family, the Browns, volunteered to offer me off-campus hospitality and assistance.
>
> Louise Brown, an Alabamian, was the friendliest and kindest adult white person I had met; she and her husband helped me solve my initial problems in understanding where to go for different needs and included me in their family gatherings . . .
>
> Finding Mrs. Brown, with her thick southern accent, to be the antithesis of a racist shamed me into recognizing my responsibility to avoid relying on the same kinds of stereotypes that had so long imprisoned me and my family.[13]

Mrs. Brown gave Ruth hope. Something she has never lost.

She found a life in academia, eventually becoming president of multiple major higher education institutions, including Smith College, Brown University, and Prairie View A&M University. She

13 Ruth J. Simmons, *Up Home: One Girl's Journey* (Random House, 2023), 176.

was still aware that people often treated her differently—as a Black woman, they tiptoed around her. However, Ruth found a few people who didn't shortchange her of opportunities to grow by telling her the truth, pushing her to work harder and to be more critical of her own work—and not to expect any free rides. Whatever she hoped to achieve, she would have to earn in her own right to bring to reality the world she imagined back in East Texas. Today, Ruth is one of the most distinguished educators of our time, with more than 40 honorary degrees from universities worldwide, including Oxford, Harvard, Brown, Princeton, Dartmouth, and the University of Toronto. All because people early in her life pushed her to continue to be the best she could be and gave her hope for a different world. And, in turn, that is something she has given to thousands of students.

Dr. Ruth Simmons

Dr. Ruth Simmons, a pioneer in higher education.

Consider the work of Dr. Laura Kleiman, who was working at the Dana-Farber Cancer Institute running a center that was focused on using AI and data science to help treat patients when her mom became a cancer patient herself.

Laura began furiously figuring out treatment options for her and came across an opportunity to repurpose generic drugs as a way to get new and affordable treatments to patients faster than any traditional drug development approach.

She learned quickly that there is no pathway to bring these types of drugs into the standard of care—the existing drug development system does not contemplate discovering new uses for existing generic drugs, and pharmaceutical companies have no economic incentives to develop and sponsor these existing drugs for new uses once their patents expire. And yet, 10 million people die from cancer each year and nearly 40% of American patients exhaust their life savings within two years of diagnosis, with 25% delaying their care because they can't afford it. Sadly, despite Laura's herculean efforts, she couldn't save her mom. But the experience redoubled her efforts to save all the other mothers who had cancer and could still be saved.

Dr. Laura Kleiman, Reboot Rx

Dr. Laura Kleiman with her mother, Fran David-Sontag, in November 2012.

She took what she had learned and created a proprietary data model that analyzes published data on generic drugs to identify how they can quickly be repurposed to be used to treat other cancers at a fraction of the cost of non-generic drugs, often because they have already gone through Phase 1, 2, or even 3 clinical trials for the cancer treatment hypothesis!

Today, Reboot Rx is showing early promise in three different cancers. All because Laura turned her grief into hope and her hope into action so that cancer patients might have a different destiny than her mother.

Francis Nderitu grew up on a fish farm in East Africa where his parents struggled to make ends meet. During the rainy season, markets were not accessible and much of the fish and produce they would normally sell for income would spoil and had to be thrown away. But instead of accepting the situation, Francis used his training in technology and computer science to find a storage solution for smallholder farmers, one that would streamline and improve productivity and efficiency in order to be more competitive. Today, Keep IT Cool, the 2024 Earthshot Prize winner, provides proximate refrigerated cooling boxes and transport to smallholder fishers and farmers across East Africa. Their end-to-end cold chain logistics solution matches fish and poultry supply to the demand of rural and urban customers, impacting more than 250,000 livelihoods and creating increased economic opportunities for more than 64,000 fishermen and farmers.

Keep IT Cool

Keep IT Cool provides sustainable refrigeration and delivery solutions for small farmers across Africa, boosting livelihoods and reducing spoilage.

Sherry Riva is the poster child for harnessing endless empathy and hope and turning them into action. She was focused at an early age on anti-poverty and domestic violence work related to women and families. At 29, she became the executive director of a transitional shelter for women called Jubilee Women's Center in Seattle. The main residential program was located in a beautiful old convent that became a home for 30 women who were homeless or at high risk of becoming homeless. Being up close and hands-on in her role, Sherry observed over and over again the cycle of poverty that traps so many women and their families. She was obsessed with finding solutions that would do more to help women and their families move up and out of poverty.

A few years later, Sherry moved to Boston and by chance came across a paper by a finance professor at HBS, Peter Tufano, who had written about the check-cashing industry, a predatory financial service, and documented what the average consumer of check cashing could have saved over their life had they not used check-cashing services—it was equivalent to a down payment on a median-priced home. Tufano's work, along with the groundbreaking 1991 book *Assets and the Poor* by Michael Sherraden, led Sherry to thinking about the idea of asset-building as a way out of poverty. She realized that poverty wasn't just an income problem; it was an asset accumulation problem. In fact, the very programs designed to help low-income people meet their daily consumption needs—programs like food stamps, housing subsidies, and welfare payments—fail to support or incentivize saving. Most of these programs actually create "disincentives" or "asset limits," which means that people will lose their benefits if they save above the allowed threshold. As a result, these systems, which were intended to alleviate poverty, often create "poverty traps" that make it nearly impossible for people to get ahead.

Inspired to take action, Sherry enrolled an initial group of nine families in Roxbury, Massachusetts, into an innovative matched savings program designed to help people achieve their goals and dreams—like buying a home, starting a business, or saving for their children's education.

This was the beginning of Compass Working Capital. Sherry knew she was onto something as interest in her work took hold and the organization grew quickly. Most importantly, Sherry began to see the impact her work was having on people. In her tireless search for scalable asset-building solutions, Sherry then identified an existing federal housing program, the Family Self-Sufficiency (FSS) Program, that created powerful savings opportunities for families in federally subsidized housing—people like Damali, a mother of three who has spent the last two decades learning, saving money, and trying to get ahead. Damali had her first daughter when she had just graduated from high school. With little assistance and resources, she worked extra hard to get her bachelor's degree while raising her child, but was barely getting by. At age 40, Damali became pregnant again and had no other choice but to apply for public assistance. But Damali wanted more for herself and she was resourceful, so when her sister told her about the FSS program, she enrolled. Today, Damali is a proud homeowner in Boston through the Compass FSS program. "This type of program is the pathway out of poverty,"

Damali said. "Without a program like this, oftentimes it's absolutely impossible to save because you're literally living paycheck to paycheck." At the time it was a powerful but underutilized program, with an estimated 2.2 million households eligible to take advantage of the program and change the trajectory of their lives.

Today, Sherry and Compass Working Capital have given hope to more than 6,000 people across 15 states who have collectively saved more than $27 million, ending the poverty trap that had constrained them, all because one person cared.

Compass Working Capital

Damali pictured with her children in
their new home made possible through
Compass Working Capital's FSS program.

These are not isolated examples. They are out there if you look hard enough. In the previous chapters of this book, I have given you example after example of one human being giving hope to others and making a difference in the life of another. My wife, Nancy, adds another dimension to this narrative.

Because more than any other person I have known, she has an unrelenting approach to accepting what life hands you, never giving up and rarely losing her capacity to see joy and meaning in everyone. It's centered in her core belief that we only get one shot at life and, regardless of the cards you pull, you better appreciate every day you get because you never know if it's your last. So she lives life to the fullest; even when despair tries to slow her down, she continues to live fully.

After 83 chemo cycles, 291 doctor appointments, multiple trips to the emergency room, more than five different hospital stays over four years, and two clinical trials, she remains undeterred. In between chemo treatments that took place every three to four weeks for the past four years, she often went on bike trips with me, played pickleball and tennis, went out with friends even as hair loss set in, traveled with me monthly to visit our daughter, and was there for the births of our three grandchildren. She took as little time as possible to rest and recover from chemo or surgeries. She didn't want to waste a day of living, enjoying every moment. She still did everything she needed to manage her health, but didn't shy away from actively living with enthusiasm, pursuing passions, staying true to herself, and finding joy and meaning in so many experiences.

She is the perfect model for quiet gratitude for what she has, not what she has lost.

On at least three different occasions over the past four years she has been given a prognosis that gave her a few months—even a few weeks—left to live. And throughout it all, she was never angry, never screamed at the cosmos, never felt sorry for herself that her life suddenly changed and was often full of pain, because that would be wasted energy and, more importantly, wasted time.

Nancy is the epitome of hope. She embodies and inspires hope, demonstrating unwavering optimism, resilience, and a belief in a better future even in the face of adversity. She did this when our son, Peter, died. She did this when she was diagnosed with cancer. She continues to do this today.

And I am reminded every day of that fall day in 1981 when Nancy and I repeated the words so many couples do when they get married: "I promise to love you and care for you through sickness and in health till death do us part."

No one gets a free pass in life. What matters is what you do when called to act. I know firsthand that the love I have gotten has exceeded anything I could have given.

And the Nancys of life are everywhere if you look hard enough.

I have seen these transformative everyday human beings change the course of others' lives hundreds of times through my work at DRK, where we see hope triumph in the leaders of organizations working in complicated and often dangerous environments who see inequity and lean in. They see constraints that hold people back and give their heart and soul to free them. They see the world as it exists but refuse to accept it. They don't let the status quo define their future or their destiny. And they ask for nothing in return. No fame, no glory. Just the ability to make a difference. More than that, embedded in their hearts and their souls is the fundamental belief that change can happen. It's a powerful reminder that in a world where hope is in short supply, there's plenty of it right in front of each of us if we only grasp it.

You just have to be open to see it, to feel it, and to take it in.

And it's not just in the hands of a few, but in the hearts of many. It only requires one thing—for you to act.

Epilogue: The Future Is in Your Hands

"Never underestimate the power of hope."

—Jim Bildner

Throughout this book, I've shared how several DRK social entrepreneurs found and recognized hope in their own lives and then used that hope as a tool to set a course of action to change the lives of others. It's what drove them to risk everything for an idea that others said, as the sheriff told me, was too big and too impossible to fix. It's the same thing that drives communities to rebuild after tragedy strikes.

Through their stories, and through the stories of some of the hardest moments in my own life, I hope you can see yourself and the power within you.

You don't need to be a social entrepreneur to create change and give hope. You don't need superpowers or super resources or super access. All you need is the belief in humanity's ability to make a difference in the lives of others, starting with you and what you do to make a difference in your world and the world around you.

Everyone has the potential to make a difference.

I see it firsthand, all the time, in the incredible care that Nancy's nurses and doctors have given her—and me—over the last five years, and believe me, their jobs are hard and often thankless. I see it in our own team, spread out around the world, facing their own challenges in their personal lives and in our work on the front lines of securing the safety net. The work is unrelenting and so are the challenges that inevitably take hold in their personal lives. But they show up every day knowing that they are making a difference in the lives of others and, in return, feeling in their very hearts and souls that this act of service—translating their hope into action—completes their own lives.

This isn't some wishful belief. It's real. So, wherever you are in your life, your career or whatever you do, or where you live, the opportunity is right in front of you. You just have to seize it.

On September 28, 1960, John F. Kennedy gave

one of his most important speeches outside the Lawrence Hotel in Erie, Pennsylvania. In that speech, he asked Americans to change the way they looked at the country. His words were simple: "Ask not what your country can do for you; ask what you can do for your country." Today those words continue to resonate, but not merely in the context of a single government. They are a call to action for each of us to do what we can for our world and for each other.

The other night, I heard a performance by Renée Elise Goldsberry, who sang a compilation of songs from *Rent*, including "Another Day." The message says it all:

It's up to each of us.

The time to act is now.

Hope gives you the power to change someone else's life, and in that very act, to change yours. It's there for the taking. You just have to accept the challenge. Like the ripples from a single drop of liquid landing on water, one person's decision to act to make a difference in the lives of others can multiply exponentially, creating more change than ever imagined.

I know because I have seen it happen over and over again. This belief changed my life for good, and I know it can change yours.

What you do with it is up to you.

The time to act is now.

Jim Bildner

Jim and Nancy Bildner set sail on their boat *Copacetic* in 1981.

Acknowledgments

For some, it might take a village; for me, it took a city. I want to acknowledge a number of people for all they did, some knowingly, and some who never knew what I learned from them.

First, my parents, Allen and Joan. My dad was truly legendary for his kindness, his heart, and, above all else, his seemingly endless reservoir of care for others. Growing up, watching him at work as he ran our family supermarket business, King Supermarkets, was a lesson in just how powerful simple acts of kindness can be. I will never forget spending Sunday mornings with my dad as he toured the stores. My father would meet with the store manager and I would "shag" shopping carts in the parking lot, collecting them and bringing them back into the store, then join my dad before we left the store. As we walked together through the store, my dad would stop and say hello to every store employee. He knew their names, their families, how long they had been with Kings, and any event that had just taken place.

And, of course, my mom, Joanie, as she was known. She was a force of nature, deeply caring, ambitious, not afraid of anything, and curious about the world. She was also the disciplinarian in our family responsible for putting guardrails around us. The same guardrails I would regularly test. She allowed me just enough freedom to learn independence without putting myself in too much danger along the way. And, equally important, my parents were role models for my brother, Rob, and me for what it means to truly care about others. During their lives, they gave their time, expertise, and money to countless institutions and initiatives, large and small, which continue to make a difference today.

I want to specifically acknowledge the impact that the late US Senator Howard Metzenbaum had on me. I served as his speechwriter for nearly two years during his first term. A very successful businessman prior to being elected to the Senate from Ohio, he defied all expectations, serving throughout his terms as a leading advocate for workers across the state and the country. As a 23-year-old, I was given a front-row seat to how to make a difference in the lives of others, how to form coalitions with people who had different, often opposing, views. He taught me much of what I know about communicating core messages and also planted the seed in me for public service, which has been an integral part of my life's activities when the opportunity has arisen. I miss Howard, his sense of humor, his mentorship, and his relentless advocacy for those in need. He literally changed my life.

And to Alex Johnson, my instructor in my nonfiction Master of Fine Arts program who taught me to write from the heart even when my heart was broken after Peter died.

To Brian McGrory, who as a columnist at *The Boston Globe* was a voice for those not heard and the eyes for those not seen. Brian, your columns are a reminder of hope and what it can do in life.

And to the *Boston Globe* home delivery driver, who at 4:30 AM on an early June 1988 morning stopped his car as he noticed someone—me—picking up every newspaper he threw out of his station wagon delivering newspapers in our neighborhood. I happened to be the feature of that morning's "rise and fall" article in the business section and was embarrassed by what my neighbors would see. His name was Connor and this was his route. He knew me by name. He said, "Jim, when I saw your name, I read the article when I picked up the papers at the Dorchester printing plant this morning. It's a good piece. Don't worry about it, and remember, tomorrow folks will be wrapping fish with it. Go home and have some coffee." That reminder to never believe your own press or take yourself too seriously has stayed with me my whole life. I give that advice to our portfolio entrepreneurs all the time.

And to Mitch Zuckoff, who taught me never to bury the lede and so much more in his class on reporting and his own writing. We lost touch along the way, but his lessons remain.

And to some of my fellow Kresge board members who, during my nearly 20 years on the board, taught me so much about philanthropy and so much more about life. They also gave me the chance to develop our Social Investment Practice and develop new tools at Kresge to transform the conditions on the ground for vulnerable communities across the country. These include Lee Bollinger, Elaine Rosen, Cynthia Kresge, Nancy Schlicting, Maria Otero, Irene Hirano, John Fry, and Suzanne Shank, to name just a few.

And to the senior staff of Kresge, including Bengy Kennedy, Amy Robinson, Aaron Seybert, Rob Manilla, Kimberlee Cornett, and, of course, Rip Rapson. My time on the board represented some of the most transformative years in my life.

And to my friends and colleagues at Harvard's

Kennedy School of Government who do the hard work, every day, to support leaders around the world and to help keep the dream alive that government for the people, by the people, can work. You all inspire me every day.

And to my friend Stan McChrystal, whose lifelong commitment to service and to character has never been more important. Thank you for showing us all the importance of standing up for what you believe in.

And, of course, to Draper Richards Kaplan. More than the names on the "door," my three senior partners, Bill Draper, Robin Richards Donohoe, and Rob Kaplan, demonstrate what caring about others is all about. They are full of heart, unrelenting in their belief in a better world, and three of the most committed human beings to take that hope and move it into action. What they started in 2002 has now become one of the most powerful forces for good in the world. Bill, Robin, and Rob, thank you for all you have done for others and for me. I would not be who I am without you.

And to my fellow DRK board members Sue Gordon, Ruth Simmons, and Judy Woodruff, thank you for all your advice and mentoring to all of us at the foundation.

To the DRK team, you are simply the best in every way, as I have described in this book.

To the DRK senior team of Nancy Huang, Zeryn Sarpangal, Anika Warren, Kathryn Shehade, Lara Metcalf, Kanini Mutooni, and Lisa Jordan, thank you for your partnership and care—it means the world to me and to the foundation.

I also want to thank Stephanie Khurana and Stephanie Dodson Cornell, who served the foundation so selflessly during their time with us.

And to the more than 90 donor partners who support our work, thank you from the bottom of my heart. The stories in this book would never have become realities without your support and care. You can find the names of these incredible people in the DRK Foundation's Annual Report.

To Ari, Clem, Kiah, Aimée, Evan, Wawira, Edith, Jared, Charles, Laura, Francis, and Sherry, thank you for letting me tell your stories.

And to our other more than 270 DRK portfolio organizations making a difference in the lives of more than 650 million people, thank you for doing what you do. You inspire the world with what's possible. You are the definition of moving hope to action.

And to my friend Carrie Morgridge, whose passion for others and relentless support of organizations around the world are proof points of how you make a difference.

And to Kristin Abati, who was always there when we needed her these past five years.

To Nancy's "A Team" of doctors, Dave Ryan, George Fisher, Hiroko Kunitake, Vicki Jackson, and Leon Pappas, and their incredible team, including Daniela Proia, who literally moved heaven and earth to schedule hundreds of doctor appointments for Nancy and me. Thank you for being there for us when life intervened. And for saving Nancy's life and, with it, mine. You were all just a text away day and night, and always reminding us to never give up hope and keep taking shots on goal.

To Ken Lizotte, my agent, thank you for believing in this project.

And to Matt Holt and the BenBella team, thank you for bringing this book to reality. You are the very best.

And a special heartfelt shout-out to Kathryn Shehade and Nancy Huang, who served as our in-house editorial team. Words cannot express my gratitude for your dedication to this project.

Thank you to Abby Crocker, who for 25 years and counting has been by my side on every new project, every new task, and every new idea. Abby, thank you for always being there and for keeping the trains, planes, and automobiles running on time.

Finally, to Nancy, Lizzie, Alex, Ruth, Ava, Grace, and Zeke, thank you for being part of my life. You inspire and anchor me in a daily reminder of the joy life brings through thick and thin. I love you with all my heart.

Jim Bildner

Index

Page numbers in *italics* indicate photos.

About the Author

Vince Tarry, iClickStudios

Visionary leader and dedicated philanthropist Jim Bildner has lived an extraordinary life marked by success, adversity, transformation, loss, and unwavering hope. As CEO of DRK, one of the largest venture philanthropy firms in the world with offices in Boston, Menlo Park, The Hague in the Netherlands, and Nairobi, Jim has seen firsthand—through hundreds of investments in social enterprises—the power of human beings to make a difference in the world. As a frequent keynote speaker, Jim is a force for good in the venture philanthropy world. His concrete lessons revealed through candid reflections, inspiring anecdotes, and practical insights on how to overcome challenges have served as a beacon of hope for so many.

In addition to DRK, he is an adjunct lecturer in public policy at Harvard's Kennedy School and his research interests include understanding the role of philanthropic and private capital in solving public problems. Jim is a frequent contributor to numerous publications, including the *Stanford Social Innovation Review.*

Among his many board affiliations, he was a trustee of the Kresge Foundation from 2005–2024 and chair of its Investment Committee for 14 years, while founding its Social Investment Practice, which, today, is one of the largest in the world.

In addition to his philanthropic leadership, he has held similar roles in the private sector and worked in and served in elected positions in government.

Jim earned his AB from Dartmouth College, his MPA from Harvard, his JD from Case Western Reserve School of Law, and his MFA from Lesley University. He is a member of the Bar of the Commonwealth of Massachusetts. In 2008, he was awarded the Dartmouth Alumni Award for service to the college and to his community. In 2024, he was named to Case Western Reserve School of Law's Society of Benchers, the highest alumni recognition of the law school.

A lifelong sailor and pilot, Jim believes true purpose in life is only found in service to others.

NEVER UNDERESTIMATE THE
POWER
OF
HOPE
The time to act is now.
Visit ITSAMATTEROFHOPE.COM for:
Stories of Impact
Resources and Tools
Execution Strategy Action Plan
Articles and Media
And More!
TSAMATTEROFHOPE.COM
Draper Richards Kaplan FOUNDATION
Join Us.
DRKFOUNDATION.ORG